CHOICES

AND

CONSEQUENCES

BOAZ I. BIVENS

CONTENTS

Boaz I. Bivens
P.O. Box 92132
Atlanta, GA 30314
Email: choices@boazbivens.com
Web address: boazbivens.com
Library of Congress Control number 2022909614
ISBN 978-0-578-37706
Printed in the United States of America
Cover and Book Designed by The Bernard Group LLC
Cover Photography by Michael Justic Hollywood Headshots

All photos in the insert courtesy of the author unless otherwise noted
First Edition

PREFACE

I first met Coach Bo in 2010 at Jarvis Christian College. We were both new employees there and became acquainted through the recruitment process of student athletes. After learning we shared a common alma mater, Grambling State University, we became really good friends and have supported each other's careers ever since.

As a colleague, I've always known Coach Bo to be a hard-working professional who has dedicated his life to education, coaching, and mentoring. I believe his impressive resume will attest to that fact. Moreover, he consistently demonstrates empathy with everyone he engages with and has a servant leadership spirit which, in my opinion, makes him a unique individual.

As a friend, Coach Bo is compassionate, kind, and willing to help no matter the situation. What I appreciate most is his loyalty, honesty, and ability to see and understand things from others' perspectives. Furthermore, he is a great direct communicator, and his positive attitude is contagious. Oh, by the way, he likes to have fun too. Over the years, we've maintained an ongoing friendly rivalry with regard to him being an Omega and me being a Kappa man.

All in all, I cherish the bond we have created for nearly a decade. I consider him a brother from a different mother. And, I must add that in an age of false generosity, negativity, and an overall ethos of indifference, it is refreshing to have a friend who not only embodies a spirit of concern, compassion, and care but who is willing to share this spirit with others. Coach Bo, all I got to say is thanks for being a great friend!

Dr. Robert C.K. Harper
Founder-Chief Executive Officer-Change Agent
The Hope Initiative

FOREWORD
CHOICES AND CONSEQUENCES

As the sun rises each day, we all have CHOICES to make. By the time the sun sets, we sometimes face the CONSEQUENCES for each one of our CHOICES. There is no question that God is the "Ultimate Decision Maker" and "Consequence Giver," but He allows us to navigate through our daily lives and paint a picture of what we want our lives to look like or how they should not look.

Keeping that in mind, we know there are people in our lives who either want to paint our picture for us or give their interpretation as if it were gospel. Each of us has more than enough happening that we should only have time to focus our attention on the brush and canvas of our own portrait. Regardless of what others think, say, or believe, you make your own CHOICES and reap the resulting CONSEQUENCES.

I was inspired to write this book to enlighten, inform and empower others to be keenly aware of their daily choices.

ACKNOWLEDGMENTS

This book is dedicated to my loving grandmother, Lena May Bivens, who prayed and molded me into the man I am today, along with my mother, Lauretta Bivens, and aunt, Marlene Burley. I would also like to thank my siblings, godchildren, and extended family, for the impact that you have had on my life.

To my former teammates and classmates, I hope you know I gave you EVERYTHING I could to make you a better player and a better person. My desire is that you will take a piece of what you learned from me and pass it on to others. I love each one of you, and there are parts of you in this book as well. Finally, to my beloved fraternity, Omega Psi Phi Fraternity Inc., my Masonic Brothers, and all the coaches I have coached with or coached for, there are parts of you in these pages as well. I cannot thank you all enough for making what I thought was impossible possible!

Thank you to my grade school teachers, who were sincere in educating me with the tools I needed to be successful. To my teachers from the street, who were sincere in educating me with the tools I needed to survive. To my street coaches who coached me pro bono and from the heart when I did not know any fundamentals of the game. To the Village that helped raise me in Brewster Douglass Projects (BDP) on the East Side of the Motor City, I appreciate all of you from the bottom of my heart and the depths of my soul. And for those who are no longer with us, may your souls rest in peace. I know I cannot acknowledge everyone individually but thank you to everyone who has had a profound impact on my life. You know who you are.

Finally, to my children, you have taken the torch from my grandmother and prayed me into the father that I am today. You mean EVERYTHING to me. I know I have not always been the greatest father, but I want nothing but greatness for you. I cannot thank God enough for blessing me with the *greatest gift* that can be given to man, and that gift is fatherhood!

The following pages are inspired by the events of my life. Dealing with consequences allows us to navigate through our daily lives and paint a picture of how we do or do not want our lives to appear. However, we all know individuals who want to paint our picture for us or give their interpretation of us as if it were gospel. All of us have enough going on in our personal lives that we must each direct our attention to the brush and canvas of our own portrait. Regardless of what others think, say, or believe, every individual must make his or her own CHOICES and reap the resulting CONSEQUENCES.

"People come into your life for seasons and reasons, but a person like Bo is one that you will never forget. I am so glad that he is in my life and has been for over thirty years."

— RODNEY "POOH" GRIGGS ENTREPRENEUR
LOS ANGELES, CA

CHAPTER ONE

CHOICE OF LIFE

LIFE IS A CHOICE, not a guarantee! As humans, we only participate in the physical act of conceiving, but God plants the actual seed, and from there, life is formed. He gives us a choice as individuals to engage in the act of consummation. I remember a moment from my young teenage years when my uncle was in a heated argument with his adolescent son (my cousin). As they elevated their voices to disrespectful tones (I am not sure why an adult would be arguing with a child), my uncle shouted, "You should be glad that you are here because I could have splattered you on the wall." For some reason, this incident has stuck with me. Now, as an adult, it is clear that my uncle made certain choices; The CHOICE to have intercourse, The CHOICE not to use protection, The CHOICE to keep it in, and The CHOICE to name his son after him.

The statement, "I could have splattered you on the wall," is deep, and here is why. That is a true statement because as he felt the sensation coming, he could have pulled out, turned toward the wall, and let it go, and my cousin would not be here. As my thoughts go a little deeper, he chose to say, "I could have splattered you on the wall," which probably was the hardest surface in the area at that time. He did not say, "I could have splattered you on the comforter or pillow," which leads me to believe he was terribly upset at that time and wanted my cousin to feel his anger. Moreover, who says that to their child?

Consequently, men have a CHOICE in the outcome of conception. Most people feel that women are the only individuals with a choice when pregnancy occurs, based on the previous paragraph. Men have a CHOICE to consent, strap it up, keep it in, or pull it out prior to the ultimate volcanic eruption. Most adults know that it takes three to create a life, man, woman, and God. Not many know that God is the only one who can make the possibility of life a reality. So many of us take life for granted when we do not take advantage of the many gifts and talents that lie within us. Our genetics, along with God's vision and purpose, makes one's life creation perfect. From plants to trees, ants to animals, and from fish to flowers, a CHOICE was made by God to create those different forms of life.

Life is beautiful. Think about every walk of life around you and that there is some form of beauty in it that was a CHOICE. For this reason, I am not in favor of abortion because I know God would not have touched the womb of a woman if he did not have a plan for that seed. Whether through artificial insemination or natural conception, those lives were CHOSEN with a purpose in mind. I believe the lives that are taken due to abortion are not given an opportunity to be great for more than just themselves. Great in the sense of being the first in their family to graduate high school and perhaps college, and perhaps the first to make a name for their family like King, Ali, Obama, or even Bivens.

I understand that there are circumstances that may warrant an abortion, such as rape, incest, or the mother's health. Conversely, there are women who are unable to conceive and would die to become mothers. There are alternatives to abortion, such as adoption, signing over parental rights, and more. It bothers me that some men have truly little say when it comes to the CHOICE of abortion. And there are other men who encourage abortion.

I heard a story about a young lady who was involved with an athlete during college, and he had no knowledge that she was pregnant, nor did he have a say in the matter. The way he found out was bizarre; he was coaching a basketball game in her hometown and had invited her to attend. She attended the game with a friend. After, the pair were conversing while watching some kids play, and he made a comment about a little girl being extremely cute, and her reply was, "Yes, we would have had a pretty baby also." He replied, "Would have?" She then proceeded to tell him that she had gotten pregnant during their time together, but she knew he already had a child and he was in a relationship. She did not want to raise a child by herself, knowing he was not going to leave the mother of his child to be with her.

He was devastated to hear that because he did not have a say in the matter. She had made the CHOICE for them both. After he had time to think, calm down, and reflect, he realized that her CHOICE was the best one for her at that time. The CONSEQUENCES of the CHOICE they made to not use protection could have resulted in detrimental circumstances. What if she had decided to keep the child? That would have left him with some real CHOICES to make. He would have to tell his woman that he had a child on the way by another woman, then he would have the responsibility of feeding two mouths in different area codes.

Would he still have married the mother of his first child and not have the other two outstanding gifts (Children) from God, or would he have left his daughter and her mother to become the father of a child that came from a poor CHOICE? I know that this guy is not the only one who has had or is dealing with a situation like this. I will never profess to be perfect, far from it. I have made some extremely poor CHOICES in my life, and I know there are more to come. But if I can help someone along the way to make better decisions, I am willing to build this bridge for them.

The last example I want to share on this topic is one where women think the situation out a lot further than men. Men sometimes only see the trees, while women can often tell us what kind of tree it is and where it came from. I do not necessarily agree with the

CHOICE that was made by the young woman, but I respect it. As men who do not think with the correct head, we should have greater admiration for those women who do.

I am not sure if you thank God each time your eyes open, but there is someone, somewhere, who unfortunately did not open his or her eyes to enjoy life for just another day. To experience birth is the most beautiful thing imaginable. To know that a woman has nurtured a living being within her womb for nine months, and in some cases sooner. One of my sisters was premature, weighing only two pounds and thirteen ounces. The doctors informed us that he was not sure she would make it, but God had a different plan. She is healthy today and the mother of two beautiful, intelligent, and motivated girls.

There is no question that a story like my sister's is in nearly every family where life has changed life. God granted life to my sister, and that changed our family's lives. In relationships, both good and bad, the birth of a child has brought a couple and a family closer, even to the point of marriage. The birth of a child can sometimes cause a wedge between a couple for several reasons:

1) The father IS NOT the boyfriend or the husband, and possibly a one-night stand or an old flame.

2) The mother IS NOT the girlfriend or the wife, and maybe a one-night stand, or an old flame, or just looking to get paid!

3) Maybe neither of the two wanted kids and were happy without being parents or did not want to take on the responsibility of motherhood/fatherhood.

4) For example, the family is struggling financially but breeds dogs, and a special one gives birth to eight puppies. The birth of the eight puppies allows the family to sell them for $2,000, which results in them earning $16,000 from one birth.

5) A surrogate mother gets a big payday by giving birth for a family that is unable to conceive. As a result, both parties are blessed.

Life is a beautiful thing regardless of how you look at it because, ultimately, the CHOICE was from the Creator. There is life given every day, and regardless of how one may view it, life became life for a reason. There is no question that we all have a purpose, and it is up to everyone to figure out the purpose of his or her life. The CHOICE of LIFE is not only in the human form but also in animals, plants, harvests, or insects. People also give birth to visions, goals, and aspirations. If you are not feeding and nurturing your visions, goals, and aspirations, then they will never come to life.

Individuals must know that certain qualities that live inside of them are waiting to be birthed, understanding that it may take longer than nine months while not allowing it to become a *still birth*. This book was inside me for quite some time, and now you are reading it... LIFE IS FORMED!!

When I think of Bo, I think of my brother. He's been a part of my family for as long as I can remember, so he is my brother. I can count on him to check on me and the rest of the family, and when the phone rings on a holiday, I can know it's Bo without looking. But it's his loyalty, his genuineness, his humor, and even his voice that reminds me of my brother, Mercer. Since Mercer was one of the best dudes I know, naturally, Bo is a pretty good dude too.

— -CHIYAH LAWRENCE YOUNGER SISTER

Bo... Our mutual respect for academic and athletic excellence through hard work, discipline, and dedication has bound us with love for each other for nearly three decades. May you continue to teach, inspire and transform young men and women with your God given gifts for many decades to come. God Bless you, my brother!

Love You,

David "Rusty" Ponton

CHAPTER TWO

CHOICE OF FAMILY

ONCE LIFE IS CHOSEN, then comes the CHOICE OF FAMILY.

I believe most people understand that when one is born into a family or adopted into a family, they do not have a choice. If possible, I know I would have chosen a different family. I would have chosen two parents with professional careers who were financially stable, possessing secured savings, stocks and bonds, mutual funds, owning maybe some land with livestock, a business or two, living in a 10,000 square foot home with acres surrounding us, nice dependable cars, SUVs, boats, motorcycles, and even a private plane.

I would have chosen siblings who love and demonstrate love to one another daily. We would take annual family vacations to exotic places and historical landmarks and enjoy international holiday excursions. I would have chosen a family where everyone got along and always had each other's backs, never pointed fingers or judged one another, but that was not possible. My family chose me! Needless to say, no one can choose family unless through marriage, which I will discuss in a later chapter. Families can be very dysfunctional.

Depending on how you define dysfunctional will determine whether you agree or disagree with me. When you come to the age of understanding, someone will tell you who your mother is, the identity of your father, your siblings, that of your maternal and paternal grandparents, and possibly your aunts, uncles, cousins, nephews, and nieces. As you grow older, that initial introduction is forever embedded in your head, and it is reinforced through holidays, birthdays, and cookouts. But how do you really know that your family is your family? You can only go by what you were told and continue that mindset through life with those individuals.

I gave you an ideal situation at the beginning of this chapter. However, there are some who are born or adopted into those situations. Mind-blowing as it may be, some individuals are ungrateful, rebellious, disrespectful, and belligerent when they seemingly have everything. Who would not want that kind of situation for their family?

Honestly, I am glad my family was just the opposite, and here is why; I am extremely grateful for every little thing. I am far from rebellious, never disrespectful, and not sure what belligerent even means. My family was poor, which I did not realize until I was nearly grown. We lived in the Brewster Douglass Projects in the heart of the city. I am the eldest of four. My mom did not marry until recently, at the age of sixty. I was told that my dad was murdered when I was only two years old; therefore, I never knew him, and I have zero memory of him. My grandmother (my mom's mother) was married, but he (my grandfather) lived elsewhere. My dad's parents were married or remarried, and my paternal grandmother's husband was not my dad's biological father. I hope you caught all of that. My siblings and I all have different dads, except for two of us.

Stay with me here. My mom had me when she was a teenager, at age seventeen to be exact, under the circumstances of raising a boy in the projects with no dad or granddad present. Sound familiar? It should because, according to the Desoto Times-Tribune, 68% of African American households are headed by women. My mom is the youngest of seven; five boys and two girls. My uncles, the *men* of the family, were off doing their own thing. The eldest was in Tokyo, and the second oldest was in and out of the concrete hotel. The one after him was murdered at an early age, and I was told that he had the most promise of them all. The fourth brother joined the Navy, and it was a great choice for him. The youngest son moved to California and became *Hollywood*, flashy and fake, always desiring to be the center of attention and acting as if he should have his name in lights, which was the total opposite of how he was raised.

My only aunt on my mom's side of the family is my favorite aunt in the entire world. My eldest two uncles have the same father. My uncle, who was killed, I am not sure who his father is, and the last four were fathered by my grandfather. They did not live with us. I dare say that my grandmother was out there, but she *got it in* while maintaining the family. We have heard the saying again and again that *a woman cannot raise a man*. There are a lot of women who have and are going against the odds.

I love my maternal grandmother, Lena May Bivens, with every fiber in me! She is the one I credit for who I am today, but she told me something that shook my world upside down. She shared a story with me about twenty years ago. The following is what she said.

We were discussing family, and I asked, "Am I your favorite?"

I got no reply, so I asked in a different way.

"I know I am your favorite," I stated.

That time she smiled, but her response was devastating.

She said, "But I didn't want you!"

I was not sure what she meant, but she then went into greater detail.

"When you were one or two years old, your mother got arrested with you."

When a minor is arrested with an adult, the child becomes a ward of the state.

One of the arresting officers, who knew my grandmother, called her and said, "Mrs. Bivens, we just arrested your daughter, and your grandson was with her. Therefore, we need you to come get him, or he will become a ward of the state."

My grandmother said, "So! They can have him," and hung up the phone.

The officer called back and said, "Mrs. Bivens, are you sure?"

She said, "Yes," and hung up again.

An hour later, the officer knocked on my grandmother's door and said, "Mrs. Bivens, here is your grandson. I could not allow the state to take custody of him."

He went on to say, "When I was younger, you impacted my life in such a positive way. You are the sole reason why I am a police officer today."

So, I asked her, "Why didn't you want me?"

She said in the most heartfelt way, "I was tired. I had raised seven children, and I had enough to deal with your grandfather and your mother with no place to live. I was heavily into politics and dealing with the mayor's office and the needs of public housing. My plate was full, and I did not think, nor did I want to make time to raise a three-year-old boy who was not mine.

There I was, with no father, a mother locked up, and a grandmother who did not want the responsibility. I can only imagine if I had become a ward of the state or been placed with a foster family that only cared for me enough to get a check! I know a few people who were reared through the foster system and were adopted with both favorable and unfavorable results. Consequently, the choices that those mothers made had some positive and some negative outcomes.

My grandmother's forced decision was a choice that I would say was ordained by God. She instilled in me respect, morals, values, hard work, religion, discipline, and a perpetual passion for learning. I attended political meetings, church meetings, public housing meetings, and grown-folks porch meetings. When I say that many of those characteristics were beaten into me, I had truly little choice, if any. There I was, being raised by a 'single' grandmother and a single teenage mother. My grandfather would make conjugal visits every other weekend on *pay days*. It has been said that a woman cannot raise a man, but if there isn't a man present, who has the responsibility? The man I most looked up to was the neighborhood drug dealer. He gave me money for rent, food, and clothes and provided protection when needed. That sounds like a father to me.

When I look at the word FAMILY, I decided to create my own definition of what it means to me:

Father
And
Mother
I
Love
You

For me, I have to say it this way, *GAMILY*

Grandmother
And
Mother
I
Love
You

Foster families, where the state appoints children to live with a family that they may feel befitting for the child or children. They assign childcare workers to make visits from time to time. But how much love, nurturing, and education goes into raising a foster child? I am not sure, but what I am sure about is the resentment that each child endures at some point or another throughout their lives. Furthermore, how many products of the foster system have become parents and put their own children through the same experience?

In most cases, we want better for our children in every way. How many family members have had an opportunity to become a caregiver or provider but chose not to? On the flipside of that, some take in that family member and treat them with less love than they would give their own enemies, but they get that check from the state and spend it with jubilation. There are some cases where couples cannot conceive for whatever reason, and the alternative may be adoption. There are some people who came up through the foster care system and may choose to adopt to avoid the pain, agony, and heartbreak that they endured at the hands of the foster care system.

I am sure there are some cases where foster and adopted children were better off with those families than their own. Moreover, those individuals have success stories or testimonies to share with the world. Not to mention, there are foster parents and families who adopt that have Godly intentions where it is not about financial gain or a means to pay bills due to a lack of income. Those families know who they are, but the choice of family is complicated to the point of how close you are to your family.

When it comes to family members, they often get chances before we throw in the towel. How many times has a family member done something to you, and it was overlooked, or you forgave them right away? But when it is a friend who does something that we do not agree with, we cut them off immediately. Keep in mind, family, you do not choose, but friends, you do! The choice of friends will be discussed in a later chapter, so keep reading. I know there are cases where family has lied, deceived, assaulted, molested, raped, stole, abused, and even killed. I ask again, how much shall one endure when it comes to family? Family lies can drag on from generation to generation.

There is one case in my mind that I still am not over. Some may disagree, and I am fine with that. Until this day, it still bothers me; it is the story of Santa Claus. I know this may be humorous for some, but why not just tell the truth from the beginning? For quite some time, I believed there was a Santa Claus until I looked up at my project home ceiling, and there was no chimney to be found. If I have not mentioned where I grew up, let me say it again, The Brewster Projects, a place where there are no chimneys or fireplaces. After noticing that, I asked my mom, how in the hell does he get in? I left the hell part out, and she calmly said that he comes through the front door.

Most families still lie to their children because they feel it is harmless or it will take away the excitement of Christmas if they know the truth. Let me let you in on a secret, it is not who bought it, but it is the excitement of unwrapping a box and not knowing what is in it. That is Christmas for most. The damn Tooth Fairy, why do families lie about that? That makes no sense at all. Just give up the money in exchange for the tooth.

I used to get overly excited about my tooth being loose because I knew I would get some money for it from the Tooth Fairy. Until I woke up and caught my mother trying to be sneaky and slide my tooth from under my pillow, exchanging it for the currency. Boy, how disappointed I was when I saw her and not the Tooth Fairy, who, in my imagination, was fine with a big ole booty! The Tooth Fairy was another lie. Family will lie. Family will do whatever they think is best at that time, even if it is damaging in the years to come.

My grandfather would come by every other weekend and take my cousin and me with him to the racetrack. I am not sure if he told my grandmother where he was taking us, but we would have a good time. Afterward, we would go over to Aunt Ruth's house. Aunt Ruth had two sons named Royce and Sam. They were around our age, so we would eat good and then go outside and play for a few hours. That was the routine for several years. Over time, I recognized throughout all our family functions that neither Aunt Ruth nor her kids were ever present.

Fast forward to the repass after my grandfather's funeral. I noticed that most of my family was there except for a few. I want you to picture this, a house full of people eating and drinking, music playing with people enjoying the tunes, and the television on in the TV room. My grandmother was in the TV room, so I walked in there and asked her the following question.

"Grandma, why don't I ever see Aunt Ruth or Cousin Royce and Sam at any family functions?"

I am not sure how, but the music stopped! People were no longer talking, and the television went on mute.

She replied in her most powerful political voice, "Boy, that ain't your aunt. That was your granddaddy's girlfriend!"

My mouth hit the floor. Everyone else seemed to be waiting to hear her response to a question that most already knew the answer to. After burying her husband, my grandmother showed another side. From grief to anger due to being played by the man she loved. Who knew that my grandfather was a rolling stone or, using today's definition, had a *side piece*? Family will lie to family if they can or until someone has enough guts and courage to tell the truth.

Picture this, my grandfather is driving to pick us up and says to himself, *I am going to say to them that Ruth is their aunt and that her kids are their cousins, and I am going to let that run its course.* Damn! Not only that, but Ruth also had to be okay with it. Even worse, my grandmother already knew, and apparently, everyone else in the house did too. This family lie took me by storm because it was carried out every two weeks. How many other family lies are within my family or yours?

That was deep, or as we say, hits the bottom of the ocean. Once I came of age to understand family dynamics, I was told that I was named after my father, who was killed at the young age of twenty-one when I was only two years old. My father did not get a chance to be a father because of his criminal/street background. Consequently, his family became my family. I spent weekends, sometimes weeks, at his mother's house. My grandmother was adamant about me getting to know my paternal uncles, aunts, and cousins because, while growing up, I spent a lot of time with my mom's side of the family.

My extended family loved me because I was the only living offspring of Frederick Robinson (whose name is not on my birth certificate), who had lost his life at a young age. Furthermore, I *believed* that my dad was my dad and that his family was my family. As days turned into weeks, weeks into months, and months into years, I never doubted for one second that all of it was true until a few years ago when my aunt came home and said she felt that she needed to tell me something, since, from her perspective, I was old enough to handle it. She told me that she had just seen the man who could possibly be my father.

I was in total shock and disbelief. The true story goes like this, my mom dated the brother of my aunt's boyfriend, and my grandmother did not allow them to go out alone. They had to double date. After several dates, my mom got pregnant, but she was also dating my *so-called* dad at the same time.

While navigating through the most damaging obstacles and circumstances that I had to deal with growing up as an adolescent and through countless trials and tribulations as a young man, I desperately needed the insight, knowledge, wisdom, and love of a father or father figure. Just like I held on to the stories of a dead man whose nickname was Quick Bird. Because he was *quick* to take your woman, *quick* to take your money, and *quick* to take your life! I wore the number twenty-one throughout my young athletic career to honor the man I thought was my father.

Fast forward five years, and I get hit with this news on a Wednesday evening, after which I burned inside from anger, hatred, and betrayal. I had to speak to my mother about this, but I was not going to do it over the phone. This was a face-to-face conversation that was well overdue. A few months later, I flew to Los Angeles, and once we were alone, I finally had an opportunity to ask her about this guy who said he was my dad. She immediately dropped her head and refrained from eye contact. To my dismay, she still has not made eye contact with me. I let her know he told me that he was at the hospital when I was born. She danced all around the question to the point that I felt I had my answer.

Until this day, she still has not addressed the issue. As for him, I did call, and we met up a week later at a local diner, which was extremely awkward for me. He and I have the same complexion. He has a nice smile as well. But I could not even pretend to be as jubilant as he was. I was hurt and mad as hell.

After he told me how excited he was and how he was at the hospital when I was born, the next words out of my mouth were, "Where have you been?"

He looked at me like a puppy dog and said, "I have been looking for you, but I was not sure where to look."

I responded, "I am not that hard to find, and I have women who find me all the time. When I ask how they found me, they say, 'I Googled you!' So, if you really wanted to find me, you could have."

He mentioned that he had moved to Los Angeles, and he had lost contact with my mom and me. I asked him where he was before he moved to Los Angeles. This man said that my mom got mad at him and told him that she did not want to see him anymore. He said that when he came to the projects and knocked on our door, my uncles answered and told him not to come around again or they would hurt him.

At that moment, I knew he was not my dad/father or sperm donor because there was not a scary, shameful, or nutless bone or any other type of DNA like that running through my body. There is no way I would let a man or men intimidate me from seeing my son or being in my son's life. If anything, the story would be told to my son that your dad died trying to see you, not that scary, spineless bullshit he gave me. There is no need to take a DNA test when a man says that, and you know deep down that you would never even consider not being in your child's life. Well, there is a possibility, such as in my case, that you may not know who your biological father or mother is, so who do you love? I know there are stepfathers and stepmothers, and I will discuss them more in-depth further in this chapter.

The *Choice of Family* can be a difficult one, especially since you cannot choose until later in life who you truly call family. I am sure *my family* has numerous stories that can go on and on, not to mention the many I do not even know about. But for those that I do know, I will be sure to tell my children, so they will not be devastated or damaged, like me, later in life. Your family may be more stable, less dysfunctional, or even worse, but at some point, you will have to make a choice.

If I could define a stepmother or stepfather, I would say that person is someone who enters a family and *steps* into the role of the biological parent that is absent, deceased, or incompetent. The sacrifice is deep when it comes to the title of stepparent. When a person who currently has kids meets someone who does not, and that person is willing to put aside the elephant in the room and take on the responsibility, that speaks volumes about the stepparent's character. In my opinion, this is another extremely difficult choice because you can be attracted to someone and connect on every level, and then here come their bad ass kids. A parent's new love interest could be genuinely nice, but the children cannot stand that person because he or she is *stepping* into the role of their biological parent.

In some cases, a stepparent steps into a family, and it is a perfect fit. This is the pleasant side of stepparenting because there are some horror stories out there and times that it can be the exact opposite.

A stepparent can disrupt the deep-rooted love of the biological parent due to differing views and morals or by having a personal agenda. For example, the child or children are girls, and they take on the mindset that because their stepparent is not the biological parent, it would be fine to engage in sexual activities without, and sometimes with the parent's knowledge. What a shame, but it happens. The stepparent may also have a different way of parenting that can cause extreme tension in the home. The biological parent may have set the foundation, but the stepparent steps in with their own set of rules or conditions, and the child or children do not agree. This could result in them being either insubordinate or disobedient toward that stepparent.

In other cases, there is violence, abuse, neglect, and even abandonment. Where a seed of betrayal may have been planted by the biological parent, a stepparent can step in and overshadow the betrayal with love. That love for their mate becomes stronger than the blood running in the veins of the biological parents and biological children. The stepparent makes sacrifices and honors commitments. Their actions speak much louder than their words. Not all stepparent stories are bad.

"God uses people differently, and God uses people to impact lives in different ways. For me, he used FCA to touch and impact lives at Grambling State University, where I met Bo. His light has not stopped shining since."

— REV. QUINTON GIPSON PASTOR/FCA HUDDLE
LEADER TEMPLE, TX

F A M I L Y

CHAPTER THREE

CHOICE OF RELIGION

RELIGION IS a spiritual term that is used to describe one's faith in a higher being. It is said to be that which keeps a family together or even an individual person grounded. THE CHOICE OF RELIGION... Do we choose, or is it chosen for us? In most cases, our religion is chosen for us by the household where we are reared. If a child is raised in a Catholic household, then he or she will likely continue to practice the Catholic religion and pass it on to their children. The same is true with Muslims, Baptists, Jehovah's Witnesses, and others.

I grew up practicing the Pentecostal faith, which is considered a spiritual church that believes in the holy trinity, the Father, Son, and Holy Spirit, and that is about all I knew. Our weekly religious practice was to attend Sunday School as well as Sunday morning, afternoon, and evening worship services and Wednesday night Bible study.

I was an altar boy for as long as I can recall. My responsibility was to take care of the pastor and the altar. I had to be properly dressed in white from head to toe. In addition, I had to listen to the pastor, read and study my bible, memorize certain scriptures, and recite them when instructed. There were some rules, or better yet, laws, that I had to follow; the Ten Commandments, and if broken, I was going to hell. This was imbedded into my brain as an adolescent.

As I got older, I continued to pray on my knees before going to bed and again after my eyes opened in the morning. I would carry my bible in my book bag because I was taught that it was a sword against any evil presence that I would encounter throughout my day, or it was used as a quick study reference.

I was taught that if I continued to do these things, my name would be written in the Lamb's Book of Life, and I would be Heaven bound. I was also taught that people who did not do these things were not fit for the Kingdom. I would talk to my friends who did not attend my church or practiced a different religion, and they would say that their religion was the *only* religion. I even had a good friend named Yusuf Hollins, who I played ball with. He was Muslim, and he would share with me some of his teachings. It was the closest I ever came to the Muslim religion.

I was taught not to open the front door on Saturday mornings because *those people* would be by to hand out a magazine that I should never read. "Let them knock, and you better NOT open that door!" Still, to this day, I do not open the door. I thought Catholicism was a whites only religion because that was all I saw on television.

Malcom X, Minister Louis Farrakhan, and Muhammad Ali were the most prominent Muslims of my generation. Muslims would sell bean pies and fruit at major intersections while handing out the Final Call Newspaper. We were told to not eat pork, not have sex, and that white people were the devil. For some reason, I thought they did not have any fun. Also, I thought that only Catholics went to Catholic Schools. My understanding of religion was distorted and tainted.

Religion. Religion. Religion. From the pulpit, the preacher would say that we should not drink alcohol, smoke cigarettes and weed, or any tobacco products. In addition, we were taught to not have sex out of wedlock, to not lie, steal, use profanity or treat people bad. We were instructed to put this into practice daily. We believed that if we did these things, we would not go to hell or when Jesus came to claim his people, he would take us with him.

The devil must have been there because I would witness many of these sins being committed immediately after church, except for sex.

Consequently, I was taught to pray for those people, and I did. Religion was embedded in me so deeply that I would repent even if I thought about doing things contrary to the word of God. But, as I got older, peer pressure got stronger!

I participated in many of these so-called sins, but I continued to repent and trusted the word coming from the pulpit. I trusted that the man bringing the word was getting it directly from the Holy spirit of God until one Saturday evening when I was about fifteen years old. This is what I remember; the pastor had two teenage sons who were a bit older than me. We three boys would hang out together, playing ball and dominoes, and entertaining the ladies.

One night I asked my mom if I could go to their house and hang out with them. She gave me permission and dropped me off. Unfortunately, the boys were not home when I arrived. Shortly after I arrived, I drifted off to sleep and was awakened by an ice-cold hand touching me near my bellybutton and sliding lower toward my private parts. I instantly jumped up and opened my eyes. It was the PASTOR! I convinced myself that this was not happening and that it was nothing more than a bad dream. I tried going back to sleep until it happened again.

The pastor, the man closest to God on earth, was trying to grab my dick! My first reaction, while he was on his knees, was to break his face! But by me being so deep in religion, with my fist balled up and ready to strike, I believed that if I hit him, I would go straight to Hell! Not knowing what to do, I went into the bathroom and paced back and forth for several minutes. I decided to go back into the room, full of anger. It was close to 2:00 a.m. Keep in mind that this was early Sunday morning, meaning it was only a few hours before worship service.

While sitting on the edge of the bed, I was in a rage because I felt violated by someone I loved, respected, and honored. With sleep being the furthest thing from my mind, I sat on the bed for the rest of the night.

He came in again to see if I was asleep and asked, "Are you still up?"

I just stared at him with a look of death.

I remained in that position until morning, and he came in at approximately 8:00 a.m. and had the audacity to ask me if I was going to church!

"Hell no!" I replied.

Shortly afterward, my mom called and asked if I was up and getting ready for church. I told her no ma'am, and she asked why. I told her I did not feel well. I had no intention of telling her what had happened over the phone. After church, she picked me up, and I told her of my late-night experience with the shepherd of our church. She became furious, which was demonstrated by her antics and language.

I was still upset that I did not break his face for all the other children and teenagers who were not as strong as I was, who were violated, touched, sexually assaulted, or even molested by him. I wanted to punish and inflict bodily harm on him for all of those that were not strong enough to tell him no. I wanted to break his face and have him explain to his congregation, or should I say, *lie* about what happened to him.

I know I'm not the first that he tried to touch and most definitely not the last. I feel that if I had hurt him physically and he wound up hospitalized, it would have given him second thoughts about touching another minor inappropriately ever again. As for my mom, she was shocked about what I told her and went into a tirade for about an hour. I am not sure if she called him, but she acted terribly upset. That emotion lasted about two days.

She took a week off, and the following Sunday, she was back in church. His church! What a slap in the face. Perhaps her Choice of Religion had her bypass all the other churches on every corner in Los Angeles. On the other hand, I did not step foot into another church for at least five years. I did not understand how a pastor could preach about how he could deliver the word of the Lord through the Holy Spirit but then turn around and do something that could damage a child of God to the point of resentment. Until this very day, I am apprehensive about attending ANY church, not knowing if the pastor is keeping his hands to himself. Like the pastor in that southern state, who would care for the boys of single mothers and wait until they reached a certain age before he touched their soul."

I have shared my story with a few close friends, and they said that I need to let it go and forgive him, but that is easier said than done. I feel that he should ask me for forgiveness! At no point since this violation has he attempted to reach out to me like a man or, even more importantly, like a man of God. There is no question that I would have a little more respect for him if he had come to me and said he was totally wrong, or could I find it in my heart to forgive him, or something like that. Isn't that how religion or being a Christian works? I believe that if the person who is violated, wronged, abused, abandoned, or diagnosed because of what has happened to them is encouraged, instructed, baited, or asked to forgive the perpetrator for what they did, whether religious or not, these actions are almost as tragic as the incident. I personally may not accept the apology, but the fact that an effort was made could have had a positive effect on me.

I have seen this pastor one other time since that incident, ironically at a church, where my mother asked me to attend because she was speaking at their program. He had the audacity, nerve, and courage to extend his hand to me to shake. I just looked at him as if I were in that same room where he attempted to sexually assault me, and I told him to get away from me before I spat in his face. I still want to break his face. I have absolutely no love for this man, and I couldn't care less if he died a gruesome death.

The bigger picture is that I was an adolescent teen who was courageous enough to not allow a sexual predator, better known as a pastor, to violate me. Also, I was strong enough to tell the one person who should have been my protector and advocate. Unfortunately, it felt like a slap in the face when she did absolutely nothing to protect me. What is worse is she continued to attend his church. I am still devastated, damaged, bitter, and angry.

I have read stories where Catholic priests have done similar acts to young boys in their churches. I am not sure how they have endured while becoming adults, but I am not over it. I will always act when it comes to protecting my children, religious or not. Consequently, I did get enough fortitude to ask my mother why she continued to attend that man's church. Her response was that she talked to my grandmother about it, and my grandmother told her to pray about it and continue to serve under his leadership. Do you believe that? I certainly do not! I said to my mom that out of all the times she did not listen to her mother, this is the situation she chose to do so. I guess that's how religion works.

Once I attended college, I visited various religious services, including Baptist, Catholic, Jehovah's Witness, Muslim, and non-denominational. Currently, my choice is that I refuse to claim a denomination. Once again, our CHOICE OF RELIGION begins in the household that we were raised. I have come to realize that I am a living testimony of how one chooses to worship. Where and when is a personal and deliberate choice. I never criticize a person when it comes to religion because I do not know what they have been through.

The personal relationship can be considered one's CHOICE OF RELIGION. It bothers me when religious folk judge those who do not attend church or worship as they worship. Who are they to say, "You need to be in church," or the most common phrase, "You need Jesus."? When things are not going right in a person's life, the first thing a religious person says is, "You need to get right with God," or "You need to go to church more often." But when trials and tribulations occur in the life of a religious person, it is a test of their faith.

It has been my experience that some of the biggest sinners and hypocrites are under the roof that they call church.

Most gossip that starts in the church is carried into the streets. The church is supposed to be a safe haven where people can go to release their cares and those things that are heavy burdens on their hearts. It is a place to get guidance, comfort, and love. How can one want to go to that place when they are not greeted at the front door or even acknowledged by the Pastor?

Religious folks are fakes. They wear a mask, some even a double mask. Some smoke, snort, swallow, snitch, and smile all in one setting. Most of them say one thing and do something totally opposite but tote a bible and smile. Something else I know is this, there are many different churches, large, small, and some in between. Also, religion today is based on how much money you make and how much you tithe weekly, monthly, and yearly. To some, the amount of your tithe means that you are abundantly blessed and that the person who does not tithe on a regular basis or give the required amount is not living right.

Religion should not be based on finances, but in some circumstances, unfortunately, it is. If you are financially secure, you are considered blessed and highly favored. If you are not, you need Jesus. But the book says you cannot take anything with you and that God looks at the heart.

Whatever your CHOICE OF RELIGION, do not allow a person in a pulpit, storefront, garage, basement, or television to tell you how to live. Find it for yourself because, ultimately, the CHOICE OF RELIGION is yours and yours alone.

Coach Bo has been one of the most influential and impactful people in my life. He is impact does not just stop on the basketball court, but it spills over into life.

He instilled so many life gems as a coach that I live my life with a certain level of excellence, as if he is still watching me from the sidelines. I am forever grateful to have been under his leadership.

Thank You.

— PARIS MCCARTHY HEAD GIRLS BASKETBALL
COACH ROMULUS HIGH SCHOOL

Pops, I just want to let you know that I greatly appreciate you. I thank God for you daily. Thank you for being there for me the way you do. Thank you for not judging me or making me feel bad for the mistakes that I have made and am going to make. Thank you for just being you. You have made such a major impact on my life, so now you are stuck with me for eternity. I love you, and do not ever forget that.

— ADRIANA WRIGHT FORMER CRIMINAL
JUSTICE STUDENT CLARK ATLANTA UNIVERSITY

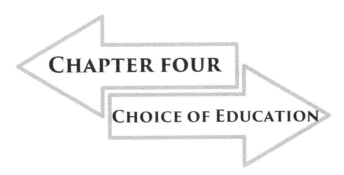

CHAPTER FOUR

CHOICE OF EDUCATION

THE CHOICE of education can be extremely difficult and stressful. Choosing a public school vs. private school, Catholic school vs. charter school, or boarding school over home schooling, two parents making this important choice for their children can be overwhelming and can be even more daunting for a single parent with multiple kids. This may sound like a promo for an educational institution, but most parents want their child to have a positive, life-changing, or life-altering educational experience.

Parents want their children to be in an environment that will teach, educate, nurture, and inspire. There are many factors that go into making an educational choice; one is location, something possibly close to home or close to the parents' job. Some parents take into consideration if there is an after-school care program. Are extra support services offered? These are just a few questions or concerns.

I am a product of the Detroit public school system, one that, in my opinion, was decimated. Though the choices of education may carry some validity, I am a solid believer that the choices of education start in the home. If a parent teaches study habits that require and demand discipline along with positive reinforcement, children will be conditioned to study regardless of what school they attend. Parents who choose to make sure their child(ren) ascertain the information they learn by reviewing with and quizzing them ensure that their children will have a much better attention span in the classroom and a better understanding of the current lessons.

Education starts at home! The dinner table is a good place for parents to make sure that children completely understand their homework and possibly understand it to the point that they can teach their parents. Discipline and education go hand in hand. If children are required to turn off their phones and not watch television when they get home from school, eliminating those distractions will help them with comprehension while doing their homework. This type of discipline instills the foundation for long-term study habits with positive results. This type of discipline requires that parents come home from a long day at work and change hats from employee to educator.

Parents should work to make sure homework assignments are completed and understood. It is understandable that the dual role of parent/educator can be exhausting, but instilling good study habits into children at early and impressionable stages in their lives will carry over into adulthood.

There are occasions when a child needs extra attention with their work, but parents are clueless or not familiar with the equations or material in which the child is having trouble because we do not take the extra time to keep up with equations or the material that is being covered at that time. We tend to put that responsibility on the teachers. Everyone knows that teachers are overworked and underpaid. It is sad when an athlete can shoot a ball, catch a pass, hit a home run, and potentially make millions of dollars while their educators make pennies in comparison.

Pre-school, primary, and secondary school teachers not only educate those athletes, but instill discipline, teach them manners and morals, and spend time with them before and after school to help them matriculate from one grade level to the next. The real tragedy is that our society values entertainment over education. As an educator myself, I speak from the heart. There is nothing more gratifying than to pour knowledge into young minds and then witness their growth and success as they conquer life challenges by using the knowledge and intellect that was imbedded in them. The choices of education extend to post-secondary as well; public or private, Ivy League or Historically Black Colleges and Universities (HBCU).

There is a strong misconception that Ivy League graduates are better prepared for the real world than HBCU graduates because Ivy League schools are PWI (Predominately White Institutions). For example, a Harvard student earns a bachelor's degree, while another graduate earns a bachelor's degree in the same field from Jackson State University (JSU), a Historically Black College or University (HBCU). They both apply for the same job. It can be preconceived that the Harvard student will get offered the job over the JSU student just based on where the students earned their degree. From my perspective, it is not where the degree was earned but how the graduate applied themselves and how well each one performed in the interview.

Where knowledge is obtained is only a small part of how successful one may be. Post-educational success requires working outside the classroom. Students must devote their time to many hours of study, research, and internships. A glaring difference for some is access to networking opportunities, business connections, organization affiliations, and family-owned corporations or businesses. Education and knowledge can be defined differently. Some can attend school but learn more from the streets. Learning how to read and write is one thing, but learning how to survive during a difficult time may be totally different.

Some say that experience is the best teacher. Our generation has been conditioned to learn as much as we can, so we will not have to go through what our parents, elders, and mentors went through. With this challenge imbedded into our brains, education becomes a short-term and long-term goal. After graduating with a Bachelor's, Master's, Law degree, Ed.D., or Ph.D., it is time for the job interview. You answer all the questions with confidence, meet the qualifications, and they like what you have to offer. After you shake hands, they smile and say that they will be in touch. Several days later, you get the call, and they say sorry, you do not have enough experience! Excuse me? Your thoughts are, *I have been in school, getting educated. How can I get experience if I have been in school?*

There are many young people who are potential success stories but are fearful of student loans. They cannot earn an athletic or academic scholarship or are unable to secure enough grant money. Some choose the military as the *next best thing*, where one can enlist as an active-duty participant or in the reserves, and the government will pay for their education. How nice is that? In the case of a reservist, you give one weekend a month, and the cost of your education is on them.

The choice of education can mean knowing that you need to start saving when you are younger so when it is time for college, one has enough saved to pay for tuition. Preparing early enough in life can be knowing how to get your education paid for through grants and scholarships and not having to take out student loans. The choices of education can be listening to those who have paved the way for you to become successful. Attaining an education can happen in many ways.

The choice of education can be establishing and sustaining communication with those who are decision-makers, regardless of ethnic origin. The choices of education can include identifying your interest early and reading daily. One's path can even be getting a GED, prep school, vocational school, boarding school, junior courses, trade school, technical school, carpentry, computer school, and more. There are so many choices. You do not have to attend college or a university to get an education. The choice of education is yours!

"Brotherhood may not come from blood, but you will know when it happens. Bo is my brother from another mother that I share everything with, and I mean everything. I could not have asked for anyone else to be as close as we are."

— MERCER "SLOW-MOTION II" LAWRENCE
RETIRED NAVY LOS ANGELES, CA

CHAPTER FIVE

CHOICE OF SEX

THE CHOICE of sex is not about gender but how this choice can have a life-altering effect. My choice came at an early age. As a young fellow, I would always hang out with the older guys in the neighborhood. There were always three main topics of conversation, drugs, sports, and sex. During my adolescence, sex wasn't a subject that we discussed in the home. It was not on television as it is today, so the street is where I learned how to kiss, what it feels like to be inside a woman, what women do with their mouths, and what women would do for drugs.

The streets taught me how some women wanted to be with you sexually if you were an exceptional athlete. Once again, this is what I heard growing up. The guys talked about those things regularly. My choice came when curiosity met opportunity. I was eleven or twelve years old, and it happened when I least expected it.

My mom decided to take in a nineteen-year-old troubled teenager who lived with us for a couple of days. Because we only had two bedrooms, my grandmother occupied one room and I the other, so the young lady had to sleep in the bed with me. One night when I was headed to sleep as normal, I felt a soft tap on my back. When I turned around, she took my head and placed it on her soft but firm breasts. I could not believe how soft they were. After that, she unbuttoned her top and gave me specific instructions, "kiss and suck but don't bite." I said, "okay," and did as she requested.

Here is where it got interesting. She took my hand to put it inside her. I had no idea what was going on. All I know is that she was enjoying it. As for me, I was looking out of my bedroom window, thinking about what I was going to wear to school the next day. But as I thought about how my finger felt, my "Peter" began to grow. That was when she asked me to put it in. My eyes got big, my heart rate increased, and every sex story that I had ever heard from the older guys raced through my head.

Here I go. I put my erect "Peter" inside of her and had an out-of-body experience. It felt like nothing I could have ever imagined. Being inside of her made me feel like I was floating and flying around the city of Detroit like a superhero, with no cape, no mask, just naked! The more I pumped, the greater the feeling until I had to pee. I took that feeling into the bathroom, but when I released it, it was not urine. You can imagine the look on my face as an eleven-year-old who just experienced sex for the first time. Kool-Aid did not have anything on my smile.

After I left the bathroom, I went back in for round two. I guess I was a little surprised at how much she appeared to enjoy it. *Wow*, I thought. *I am having sex with a girl that is much older than me.* Did I mention that she was nineteen? She was out of high school, and I was not even in high school yet.

Sex had such an impact on my life that it made me mature in a way that some do not reach. Most guys at that age would be excited to share their first experiences, but I did not tell a soul until twenty years later. I kept those moments to myself, but the *aroma* was on me. Girls seemed to recognize that there was something different about me. I noticed that girls who never spoke to me before were going out of their way to speak. My walk was a little different. My voice became deeper overnight.

School went very well the day after. I hung out with the fellas after school but said nothing. After that first encounter, when I arrived home from school, I ate and watched television for about an hour before my grandmother said it was time for bed. Sex had me going to bed faster than I ever had before. Normally, when she said it was time for bed, I usually negotiated four or five times and got and extra hour, but not that day. I got in bed so fast, waiting for our house guest to get under the covers with me.

Once she lay next to me, I could not wait to hold her. I turned, and she copied, so we were spooning, and I acted like I knew what I was doing. Shortly after we got comfortable in that position, my grandmother saw us as she walked by my room and quickly shut that down. She ordered us to get separate blankets and said that if she saw us out of our own blankets, she would kill us both.

Sex at an early age caused me to look at girls differently. I felt that I wanted an older woman, probably because they were more developed and experienced. Being handsome, athletic, charismatic, and mature caused me to be in greater demand than most. Those characteristics led me to a threesome as an adolescent. One day when I was walking to the store on an errand for my grandmother, two girls I knew approached me and asked if I thought I could handle them both. Where I come from, there is an unwritten rule that women should never challenge men when it comes to sex, even if we feel that we are incapable of achieving the task at hand. Faced with this totally unexpected proposal, I told them to meet me upstairs.

I never, I mean never, went to the store so fast in my life. I dropped off the goods to Grandma and proceeded to go upstairs and prove that I was *a two women at the same time* kind of guy. There I was, experimenting with sex once again. Because of my inexperience, I would be intimate with one and then the other but never actually engage with them at the same time. They would say, "It's my turn," or "Why are you taking so long on her?" or "You did not do that with me." I enjoyed them both. There are three more sexual experiences I had that I feel are important to share with you before I dive into the meat and potatoes, or should I say, the macaroni and cheese of the choices of sex.

The first time I received head was from my high school girlfriend. She came over after several conversations about ditching school for a day of grown folk activity. The night before, we talked about the different sexual positions that we were going to do, but when she came over the next day, she said we could not have sex. There is nothing worse for a man than to get all excited by telling him about all the nasty and freaky things that you are going to do to him, only to flip the script when that opportunity presents itself. That is the point when I go from horny to angry.

Once she noticed my emotional change, she said that she could do something else instead. I asked her what. She replied to just lay back, and then she proceeded to pull off my underwear. She then started sucking my dick like a popsicle. I had never had that feeling before, and it was amazing. After pleasuring me for about twenty to twenty-five minutes, her exact words were, "I am only doing this because I love you." In my fragile state of mind, I did not know any better. This happened at the end of the school year, and I went to spend some time with my godfather that summer.

My godfather was a baller, baller. He played pro ball, and he sold drugs. When I arrived, he gave me the house rules. Do not answer the door, if you want any woman that comes over, let me know, and you can have her. With me being handsome, athletic, intelligent, charismatic, and mature, that made me a viable consolation to him.

One day I was sitting on the couch, watching television, and there was a knock at the door. A young lady came in, selected her choice of "recreation," and then left. I told my godfather that I liked her. Later that evening, she came back, and we had sex. This would happen three to four times a week with three to four different women. During sex, they would also suck my dick. This confused the hell out of me because my girlfriend, whom I had been dating for some time, told me that she gave me head because she loved me, but now I had these women who did not know me giving me head. Boy, did that affect me.

My inexperience sexually had me thinking that women only gave head to those they loved. I was totally mistaken. Another encounter involved this beautiful woman, probably the most beautiful woman I had ever seen in my life. Her name was Anya. She was someone who educated me before my time. When I told my godfather I wanted her, he said not that one. But it turned out that she wanted me too. So, I was in the room with the finest woman on my earth, and she was gentle with me. This woman made me feel like a Marvel character. Once we were done, she asked me how it was. I said it was out of this world. My godfather's roommate asked if he could watch the next time. That request sounded over the top gay to me, but he said he was interested in seeing how prolific her "rocking the mic" really was in the bedroom.

Later that week, she returned and took charge, and this fool pulled up a chair to get a front-row seat. She locked in, licking and sucking down there like it was her favorite popsicle. I was extremely embarrassed that another man wanted to watch me get my dick sucked. As time passed, I started looking at the ceiling and glancing at the television, hoping that he would leave sooner than later. When he finally left, her next words were, "I am so glad he is gone."

She then went from superhero to super nasty woman. As I neared ejaculation, which she sensed based on me becoming more tense, her next words were, "Oh, my." Then it happened. I busted the most enormous nut ever for a teenager into the air, and she jumped up and caught it in her mouth. She said, "This is good protein," and proceeded to swallow and lick every single drop. The "protein" statement threw me off, but her actions showed me that she was certainly in a class all by herself.

Sex at age fifteen was confusing. On the one hand, my girlfriend told me she only gave me head because she loved me, but these other women were giving me head, and they did not even know me. That part of sex was very confusing. Needless to say, our relationship was over when I returned to school.

My next experience was a first for me, a relationship with a virgin. Most men dream about being a woman's first, but why? I did not know. She was also of another ethnic origin. Growing up around older guys and listening to them as a youngster, they would say how nasty it was to perform oral sex or, rather, eating pussy is nasty. Young girls would say the same about performing oral sex or sucking a man's dick.

I always believed that anyone who would eat pussy, knowing that the girl was not a virgin, was a nasty individual. Because I was sexually advanced for my age, I decided to experiment with oral sex on my girl because I knew she was a virgin. I had no idea what I was doing, and she had no idea how a tongue in her pussy would feel. She loved it. From then on, she wanted me to "eat her out" all the time. For most men, sex with a virgin causes us to become overprotective, extremely territorial, and madly possessive. Being labeled as "my first" can be a good thing or a not-so-good thing.

When a man is in a relationship with a virgin, sex as the focal point can create a monster, a sex fiend, or a pest who is not mature enough to realize that he is being a pest. Several years later, when I was a freshman in college, we were still dating, but I was in a totally different state, a 27-hour drive away. Because I was her first, I knew, without a shadow of a doubt, that she was being totally faithful, and I had absolutely nothing to worry about. I called myself being true to her by not allowing myself to get involved with anyone besides B.B.J., books, basketball, and jackoff.

My older cousin asked me if I jacked off, and I said no. He said I did not know what I was missing and that doing it would help make my dick get bigger. I had always thought that in the back of my mind. The first time I pleasured myself, I thought, *this is all right*. Until this day, I think I have pulled it a few extra inches.

Concerning my high school/college sweetheart, we talked daily. According to her, all she did was go to work and go home. Very uneventful days, so it seemed until I went home for Christmas break. I had been back a few days and had not seen her. Finally, after being home for more than forty-eight hours, I got the chance to put my lips, tongue, and body on hers. I thought I had nothing to be concerned with while away at school because I was her first, but that was wishful ass thinking.

One day, when she was taking me to the gym for a game, we stopped at a light on Sixties Boulevard, a major intersection. A red car pulled in front of us like they were the 5-0. A skinny, fragile looking guy got out of the car and walked around to our driver's side window. He did not see me initially because I was in the back seat, riding like an Uber passenger. He was smiling until he saw me.

He asked her, "Who is dis nigga in the back seat?" Her response was, "Nobody." At that point, we had been together for three years, so to hear her say those words shook me up tremendously because he should have already known about me. He tried to swing on me from the other side of the car, which was senseless, so he told me to get out. I readily accepted his demand and got out to whip his frail ass.

That's when I noticed that the guy with him was just out of the penitentiary enormous. So, I used my deductive reasoning and got my ass back in the car, and told her to drive. They jumped in his car and followed us through various neighborhoods unfamiliar to me, where I did not know anyone. I realized that no man would be acting like this over a woman unless sex was involved. During the chase, I asked her who the guy was, and she said he was just a friend. The rapper Biz Markie said to never trust a girl who says that. Being from the streets, I thought about the fact that I had got caught slippin', with no heat (gun), in unfamiliar surroundings and no one to call for help.

For some strange reason, I thought that was the end for me. He had heat, he was going to shoot up the car, and I would not finish college nor get the opportunity to play college or pro ball. But the twins, Grace and Mercy, were with me. We were on a residential street when a car backing out of the driveway blocked us, and we had no choice but to stop. That was when I realized that he was not about that life. The skinny guy and his massive friend did not get out of the car. When I looked back, I saw them turn and proceed down another street.

Once my girlfriend dropped me off at home, that was the end of us. When I went back to campus, I was like a vulture on roadkill. My first college girlfriend was a sexy specimen from the Boogie Down Bronx. We went on a couple of dates before we had sex. The sex was only okay, and I constantly had proposals from other women. I could not play ball that year due to an injury, so I had a lot of free time. I chose not to act on those propositions and remained faithful to my girlfriend until one night when she asked me to go down on her.

I said, "Oh no." I just kept thinking, *that's nasty*. Plus, I knew she was not a virgin, not to mention she had dated a football player who was out there. After I said no, she got upset and wanted to leave, so I took her back to campus and returned home alone. I saw her the next day, and she acted like we were not even dating anymore. As I was walking away, I saw one of those proposals and took her back to my place. This woman was older, played volleyball, and taught me something that night.

This woman took no prisoners. You name it, she did it, and it was amazing. Afterward, she told me that sex was better when stealing it. I did not understand what that meant, so she broke it down. She said that when you know someone has someone else, and you get that one opportunity with that person, you must make it unforgettable because you may never get that chance again. The funny thing about that situation was that she knew my girl and lived in the same dormitory. The thought crossed my mind that this was some grown woman shit. The choice of sex is a life-changing choice.

During my matriculation through college, I was given a choice to take any elective course I wanted, so I chose a sociology course entitled Human Sexuality. I thought that since I was so experienced with sex, this course would be an easy A. Unbeknownst to me, I would learn much more than I anticipated. Women outnumber men in several arenas, and in this course, the ratio was ridiculous. Thirty-seven out of my forty classmates were women.

In that course, I learned that the vagina is the cleanest part of a woman's body. It is the only part of the body that cleans itself once a month, killing all bacteria within it. On the other hand, the mouth is the total opposite, being extremely nasty. Most men prefer to kiss than eat, thinking the upper lips are cleaner than the lower lips. I also learned how to make a woman cum by performing cunnilingus. That is the correct term for eating pussy or oral sex on a woman, for those who do not know.

Revisiting my earlier statement where Anya talked about cum being a good source of protein, my professor for the course went from talking about performing oral sex on a woman to performing oral sex or fellatio on a man and asked why it was good for women. I raised my hand quickly and said because it was a great source of protein. After I gave my answer, all the girls in class looked at me and either smiled or smirked. From then on, several of my classmates asked if we could get together to study for any upcoming quizzes.

One of my peers that I "studied" with, I used some of the key points from class to give her multiple orgasms, not to mention I gave her some much-needed protein. My youth basketball coach would say that practice makes perfect. I took his advice to the bedroom and continued to practice with the females in my class. I had another experience where one of my sexy peers squirted all over the sheets, the room, and my face. I also learned that women could masturbate and have an orgasm without even touching themselves. Depending on the class discussions, I would notice several women moving their legs back and forth, squeezing their clitoris for pleasure. What a choice I made with that class elective.

With the choice of sex comes the possibility of contracting a sexually transmitted disease. This is where being a college athlete can get one into trouble. Remember, I was handsome, athletic, intelligent, charismatic, and very mature, not to mention a baller. Understand that when you are a baller, women look at you a little differently. One day while in class, minding my own business, a young lady whom I saw daily sat near me for the first time. That day she looked tastefully good, and I said to myself, *she can get it*, so I proceeded to give her "the look," and she nodded.

Immediately after class, we went to my place and got right to it. The worst part of the encounter was that I only had one rubber. When I put it on and began to put that work in, it broke. I made a choice during sex. I took a chance and went in raw. She reached her climax and went back to campus. A few days later, I experienced a burning sensation each time I urinated. There was discharge in my underwear daily, so I spoke to one of my professors, and he encouraged me to go to the clinic.

I took his advice and discovered that I had contracted chlamydia, aka The Clap. The doctor took the longest cotton swab that I have ever seen, stuck it in the head of my penis, and snatched it out. As I endured the pain, he said that I would be in pain for the next few days and assured me that I would be just fine. I never spoke to that classmate again. Another choice of sex that led to an STD is one that still gets me worked up until this day.

Once a week, my friends and I would go out and have all-you-can-eat pizza at this place called Pizza Time. One night, I noticed this server who was extremely attractive with a fat ass. On that day, I noticed her watching me watching her. When I saw the way she looked at me, I acted on it.

It is said that women know either right away or shortly after meeting if they will have sex with a man. I asked her what time she got off work and if we could get together later that night. She gave me her number. I called her, gave her my address, and proceeded to prepare spaghetti. Twenty minutes later, she rang the doorbell and entered, wearing a black fitted top and some extremely tight white pants. Damn, she had ass. She sat at the kitchen table, and I served her a plate of salad as the spaghetti was still cooking.

Once she finished her salad, she asked where my bedroom was. With dinner not completed, I turned the eyes off on the stove, took her by the hand, and guided her to my bedroom. The chemistry was through the roof. I left the lights off, strapped up, and went to work. The sex was extremely intense, and it continued that way for hours. She rocked my world like she had been waiting to unleash her sexual fantasies on me. I went through not one but two packs of rubbers, and once I was out, she had to be out.

About a week later, while sitting in class, I felt an itch in my pubic area. I didn't think too much of it. My coach required every player to wear jock straps, so I thought I had nothing more than jock itch. When I got to practice, I informed my coach that he needed to make sure the managers washed the jock straps thoroughly. A week later, it was getting worse. I recall using the bathroom and noticing spots in my underwear. After looking closely, I saw something crawling on me in my pubic area. I screamed, "Coach!" He came in, looked at me, and started laughing uncontrollably. He said, "Head (a nickname he called young athletes), you have crabs, aka pubic lice. Coach then gave me specific instructions to go to the store, purchase a box of RID, and follow the instructions inside. I did exactly what Doctor/Coach ordered.

I was furious throughout this entire ordeal. How could someone knowingly have these insects crawling on them, come over to my place, and have sex with me without getting that situation taken care of prior? Who does that? I was glad that throughout all of that bumping and grinding, I did not perform oral sex on her and get those things in my goatee. That would have been worse because someone would have seen them crawling on my mouth. But the thought of seeing her again, with my mindset at the time, I do not know what I would have done. What made matters worse was that I vaguely remembered what she looked like. I remembered her body more than I remembered her face. All I know is that I wanted to spit in her face for knowingly giving me an STD.

I remember the day in 1991 when ESPN aired a public announcement about the spread of HIV/AIDS in the heterosexual community. My heart dropped because, in my ignorance, I thought that only gay white men could contract HIV/AIDS. I can honestly say that this unexpected announcement made me wonder and nervous about my choices of sex. This was during a period when condoms were used as birth control more so than protection against diseases. It was at that point that I said, if ESPN is covering it, then I can get it, and I needed to get tested.

As thoughts swam through my head, I decided to go to the library and put a list of all my sexual partners together and the number of times we connected next to their names. I felt like this was needed, just in case they asked. Thank God my results came back negative but waiting for them was the most nervous I had ever been in my life. I was then faced with the choice of sex, including the choice of STDs, because I have had my share of one-night stands, two-night stands, and relationships that have been strictly sexual.

There was one memorable experience that I had after winning a big basketball game as my cousin Rock and I were leaving the gym. We were walking through the parking lot, heading to his two-seater Mazda Z, when to our surprise, a couple of women were lying on the hood like car show models. I asked them where they were going, and their response was, "With y'all." I opened the door, and they both got in and sat on my lap as Rock drove.

Once we got to the house, he took one woman to his room, and I took the other to mine. In the early morning, they called a taxi and left. We never saw them again, or perhaps we did but did not recognize them. We did not get their names. I can go on and on about one sex story after another. The choice of sex can lead to life-changing consequences. From a one-night stand to extended relationships, sex can create another life whether it is planned or not. A one-night stand can lead to eighteen years of unplanned parenthood or a choice to terminate a life because one person or both people are not ready. Two people can be ready for sex, but not the potential responsibility that could result.

During my time in college, I was in a purely physical relationship that resulted in a pregnancy, only I did not know until the young lady shared that information with me several years later. She decided to terminate the fetus without my knowledge. When she told me the story, I was devastated because she never told me anything, and I had no say in the matter. She told me that she wanted a family but knew that I had a girlfriend at the time. She felt that I would not leave my girlfriend to be with her, and she did not want to raise a child alone. What a choice, and what could I say? She made a choice and thought out the consequences. Some may be in a similar situation but choose differently and suffer later.

Men and women can use sex for money, job promotions, job opportunities, passing grades, reduced jail sentences, political positions, collateral, bargaining tools, citizenships and visas, drugs, vehicles, and pretty much anything else that you can imagine. For example, a woman is in an entry-level position, but she is not qualified for an upper level or managerial position. The hiring executive is very intrigued by her beauty, booty, and sex appeal, so he proposes to her that she can get a promotion in exchange for a night of pleasure. He is married, and she has a boyfriend. The promotion will put her in another tax bracket. She realizes the consequences of accepting his offer. She can get out of debt, buy the home she always dreamed of, and pick up better health benefits for her and her family. She could also upgrade her automobile, all for just one night of SEX, but who is to say that the executive would keep his word?

Let's say that she agrees with his proposal. He plans the evening, but he has conditions of oral sex and sex without a condom. She agrees to this, and he keeps his word. She becomes an office manager in the corporation and is responsible for supervising over thirty employees, which allows her to gross a six-figure income and get all the things her heart desires just because of the choice of sex. Six months later, she finds out that she has contracted AIDS. Her former boyfriend, who is now her husband, finds out about the proposal and goes to her office, and kills the executive.

Because of that choice of sex, the consequences are that the executive is dead, his wife is now a widow, and the other husband is locked up, serving twenty-five years to life. The office manager now must not only live with having AIDS but also with the fact that her choice of sex has impacted so many others. To add insult to injury, the CEO of the company was informed that she was not qualified to be in her current position, and she was terminated on the spot. What a choice. This same scenario can be reversed as well.

The choice of sex is powerful. The choice of sex can be dangerous. There are times when people get bored with sex and choose to experiment with multiple partners, toys, gadgets, and even drugs, just to make sex more exciting or fulfilling. In some cases, people can recognize their sexual potential and use it to make a brand, i.e., Super Head. There is no question that there are those who target professional athletes, entertainers, movie/television stars, politicians, or even potential athletes. They have sex, get pregnant, or even get married because of the choice of sex. Some people believe that sex is better with those who have money, but it is also extremely dangerous.

One thing is for certain, sex sells. Sex is used for advertising, merchandise sales, marketing, commercials, videos, restaurant servers, nightclubs, bars, sports bars, sporting events, movies, and just about anything one can imagine. Sex kills relationships, businesses, marriages, reputations, people, and almost anything that one can imagine. One thing that bothers me is when a person is in a committed relationship but continues to have sex with someone else. Feelings can get involved, which can cause a wedge in their current relationship because they feel that the sex is better with their sidepiece.

I believe that love and sex are totally different, but love is another choice for another chapter. I am sure most of us have been in the position of experiencing some amazing, out-of-this-earth, or out-of-body sex. Some say that size matters, but others say it is what you do with the size you have that matters. Either way, it plays a major role in sexual satisfaction.

There are universal barber shop conversations about sex that often lead to questions about your worst sexual experience or bad sex. The worst encounter can be that highly anticipated one-night stand when the chemistry is as high as Mt. Everest, and the plan is in motion. You want to get it on immediately. Based on physical appearance, sexual conversation, fragrance, and maybe one's reputation, your expectations are extremely high, but then it goes down, and it is awful, the worst, and a damn shame. The choice was the wrong one but only for one person. The other person is totally satisfied and blown away by how good it was and cannot wait to tell a close friend. The satisfied person wants more, and the other person does not want anymore. For them, it was the worst. The choice of sex is strange like that.

There are some who choose to be celibate by abstaining from physical sex. What a choice. In that same vein, you have some who say they are celibate but choose to only get fingered or have cunnilingus performed on them, or give fellatio, play with toys, everything but penetration. In my opinion, when you engage in those activities, you are not celibate or a virgin, but you can continue to think you are.

So much can be said about sex and how it plays a role in relationships. For example, a couple has a child together and have both moved on with their lives, but they may still get together from time to time because of the bond they share. I cannot explain why that happens, but it is what it is. What about that always waiting in the wings make-up sex? Some would say that is the best sex. It is still a choice. When one person is mad at the other or both become mad at each other and transfer that anger into the bedroom, car, closet, basement, workplace, kid's room, locker room, bathroom, kitchen (nasty), or wherever they choose, the sex will be intense.

Sex can have so many different titles, such as make-up sex, one night stand sex, weekend rendezvous sex, an affair (sex over & over for a duration of time), just a nut, a stress reliever, a mark, a dollar, a meal ticket, a sex fiend, or just curl my toes. I know there are a lot more titles for sex, but I will leave that for you to add. Some choose to pay for sex, so they do not have to deal with all the extra stuff that comes with just getting off, like unnecessary attitudes, exaggerated foreplay, or anything extra, period. But others choose to pay for it in other ways, by buying gifts, dinner and a movie, wining and dining, Netflix and wings, travel dates, or continuous dates that require one to drive and use gas that also costs, or ride-sharing, to ultimately get that opportunity for sex. The cost of dinner, movies, and gifts could possibly total the same amount or more as it would cost to pay for sex.

The choice of sex will have a person climb through a window and climb out of another window to go get some or leave the bed with someone else to go get some. Sex will have one betray a friend, loved one, or family member just for sex. Sex will make one stop studying for an exam, miss work, skip practice, reschedule a doctor's appointment, or even leave your kids home alone, just for sex. The choice of sex will have a person choose to take a trip out of town on limited funds, get in a car, and drive three hours or more just to get some. The need/desire for sex will make one even have it with a family member, by blood or marriage.

The choice of sex can have a married or unmarried couple become swingers (consensual sex with other people they do not know or just met, and sometimes someone they already know, which may ultimately open Pandora's Box.) This can be a most exhilarating but dangerous CHOICE. I am familiar with couples who start swinging together, then one person's appetite grows larger than the other person's. In a relationship, you want to keep your mate happy in the bedroom, but there may come a time when you are unwilling to go beyond a certain point sexually, or just maybe the sex between the two has become redundant with the same routine, same position, same location, same length of time, same scent, same shower gel. Maybe for one's birthday, one may switch a position or a hairstyle. You get the picture. However, the choice of sex has its pros and cons.

Sex can be freeing, thrilling, and fulfilling all at once, but the choice is yours. Just hearing the word sex may turn some people on. Looking at someone seductively can turn someone on. Wearing certain outfits can turn someone on. Certain scents can turn someone on. Not wearing certain things (bra, panties, or hair weave) may turn someone on. Driving or riding in certain vehicles or even just traveling can turn someone on. Certain vacation destinations or certain foods, or better yet, watching someone preparing the food, can turn someone on. Watching someone fix or repair something may turn someone on. Some people may be turned on just by reading this chapter of the book. Everyone is different.

What turns one person on may not do it for the next person. Being turned on may constitute a desire or feeling of wanting to be touched or kissed in a certain way or location. That person may want to have sex but not with the person that is in one's presence. Though you are turned on at that moment, you have a particular person that you want to take you to ecstasy. That may sound crazy, but it is true.

A woman can be at a cookout, and the topic of multiple orgasms arises. The guys are having a great time with this discussion to the point of going into great detail about how many times each guy has had an experience with a woman that has climaxed multiple times. The woman is saying nothing, believing she is only listening to lies, but listening to the details of the sexual experiences is turning her on to the point that she begins to masturbate (without touching herself) by opening and closing her legs until she cums while sitting right there. Panties soaked.

From that climax, she is content and satisfied and does not want to have sex with any guy at the cookout or even in the conversation. But let us now reverse the roles. If a man is in the same conversation where women are talking about how they can make a man cum from oral sex, he cannot just sit there and be silent. He wants to enhance the conversation by saying how freaky and nasty he is behind closed doors or in public places. He wants to entice one or any woman in the conversation to demonstrate on him until he is rejected time and time again. Totally different outcome. In my opinion, women want sex just as much as men do, if not more. There is a misconception that men stay horny, and women do not think about sex as much.

Women can meet a guy during her lunch hour, have sex, and go back to work like nothing ever happened, or have dinner and drinks and have the best sex ever, then never call him again. Men, on the other hand, will stay on her like a bill collector, blocked or unblocked.

The bizarre thing is how men think we know when our woman has been with someone else. We may suspect it by her body language, her clothes, undergarments, or behavior. Man, please! Not so, fellas. Women are five steps ahead of us when it comes to cheating. A woman will buy condoms, panties, and perfume on the way to get that "D" and dispose of those items on her way home.

"Bo is the kind of guy that you can love for many different reasons. Our paths crossed through working with Tom Joyner. During that time, he demonstrated his love to the guest, the crew, the cruise line workers, and most importantly, to me. I love him for who he is and what he stands for. My prayer is that I wish the world had more people like him in it."

— WARREN "DUB" BAKER ENTERTAINMENT
CONSULTANT HOUSTON, TX

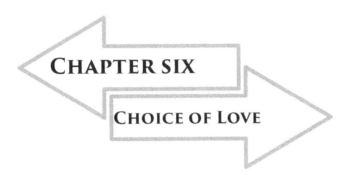

CHAPTER SIX

CHOICE OF LOVE

LOVE IS a word that is used in many ways. It can be defined in various forms. My definition of love is feeling so deeply for *someone or something that you are willing to die for that person or thing.* I know this may sound crazy to some, so let me explain. To die for someone you love does not imply that you will commit suicide. If the person you love needs a kidney, and the doctor informs you that there is a possibility you can die from donating your kidney, but you decide to continue with the procedure, in my eyes, that is a choice of love.

Another choice of love is when a pregnant woman is considered high risk, and the doctor gives her the option to terminate or continue with the pregnancy. If she chooses the latter, and from that choice, she dies on the table after giving birth, that can be considered the ultimate choice of love. If a robbery, carjacking, or any violent act occurs where one sacrifices his or her life so their loved one(s) may live, that is love!

Some people even have that type of unexplainable love for their pets, plants, insects, cars, and other material things. Most people equate LOVE with the emotional feeling that one gets when they see a certain person or are around a certain someone. Love can also be defined as how someone makes you feel inside and out, exclusive of sex. Some mistake *good sex* as love, based on how much emotion is involved or how long they have been in a relationship.

In my opinion, love should never be based on the length of a relationship. I have heard the saying *love at first sight,* but I do not believe in that. *Love at first sight,* is a direct correlation to being attracted to someone's physical appearance and loving what you see initially, but *love* is an action word, and action must be attached to love no matter how you define it. Many people say, *let's make love, or we made love,* but in my opinion, unless you are married, you just had sex.

I am sure that in your past relationships or the relationships of someone you know, the words *I cannot live without you* were spoken, but you have no idea where that person is today. Perhaps you do know where that person is, but now you cannot stand to look at them or be near them. Someone once said that *there is a thin line between love and hate.* Love is beautiful. It hurts, brings joy, delivers agony, and has an agenda. It has a path and a destination. Love is many things, but never something we can plan. Love can and will sometimes be misinterpreted as something else.

My grandmother would say to me, when it came to love, keep living. I thought I was *in love* so many times. When I was young, there were moments when I would say *I love you* and not realize that I had spoken those words until after the words spilled out. If you do not know by now, that four-letter word can hurt, damage, and scar someone for a lifetime. When it comes to love, being in love, or even displaying love, at least one person can be devastated if the relationship does not work out. The other person may not know how deeply they are loved or how painful it is for the other person to sever ties.

I apologize to anyone reading this who I may have hurt, damaged, or scarred. One of the reasons I wrote this book is that I have not always made the right choices, and I am living with the consequences of my decisions. I am awfully familiar with karma, and I know she may hit me through my daughters. If that happens, I realize it is perhaps a consequence of my actions toward others. This book is so befitting not only for me but for other readers who can relate to my message about the CHOICE OF LOVE and the CONSEQUENCES of our CHOICES. *I love you* sounds good coming out of our mouths, but once it reaches its target, watch out. God only knows the outcome.

Someone in your life might know how much you love basketball and is willing to sacrifice time out of their day to come rebound for you. Even though they do not care for basketball, they do it for you. A woman may see your potential in a way that you do not see yourself, and she does the uncommon or nontraditional thing by asking you to marry her. A woman asking a man to marry her is still rare, comparatively speaking, and that can be viewed as a true choice of love.

Love is walking into a classroom and seeing one of God's most beautiful creations, then inviting her to a cookout, and she stays the night. Love is listening to "Choosey Lover" and "Between the Sheets" by the Isley Brothers repeatedly until those songs are embedded into your memory. Each time you hear those songs, they bring back the love that was shared at the time. Love is Silence of the Lambs. Love is amazing! Love is being there for that one you love after surgery or delivery, making sure that person knows that nothing else in the world matters. Love is bringing that individual with you for the weekend of the Florida Classic. Love is cleaning and bathing that person when they cannot do it for themselves.

Love is going out of your way every single day to make sure that person knows how much you love them, Coleman Love. Love is being in a room full of people, and that person you love seemingly descends from heaven like an angel. Love is meeting someone for the first time at a pizza bar and you share your food with them, never wanting to leave. Love is displaying your feelings in twenty-two different ways. Love is sacrificing your job for the rehabilitation of someone else to make sure they follow the recommended instructions for a full recovery. Whenever you are not working, you are nursing them back to health.

Love is sacrificing your physical self and your mental health for family. It is recognizing and acknowledging the difference between love, lust, and great sex! Love is knowing without a shadow of a doubt that God placed someone in your life at a certain time for you to experience *true love*. Love comes in many different forms.

You may need someone to love you spiritually, love you enough to pray for you daily and often, or even pray for you more than they pray for themselves. You may need someone to love you enough to feed you whenever you are hungry, prepare your favorite meal and favorite dessert, like frying fish, and then sleeping with you on the floor, just because. Food and love are one, in my opinion, because cooking for someone is an expression of love. Love is in the preparation, presentation, and serving of food.

You may need someone to love you enough to believe in you and support your vision in whatever way possible. Others may need someone to love them enough to be strong where they are weak. Some people may love you enough to remove you from a situation that may hinder you from prospering. You may need someone to love you enough to stand by you while wanting nothing in return when everyone who claims they love you has turned their back on you.

The choice of love is different for everyone. The experiences of love are different for many. Love can become motivation. It can also become discrimination for some. Love can also turn into hate. In some cases, a person can love someone so much and put everything into the relationship, only to get their heart crushed. Eventually, they can no longer stand to hear that person's name. Love can turn into fear, danger, regret, and even abuse.

If God is love and He gave up his only begotten son for us, would some who aspire to love as God loves ever consider giving up their only child for someone else? There are some people who just do not know how to love people the way they should be loved. God is love, and it is a choice to love like God loves us. We tend to love with conditions. For example, we determine if someone loves us by what they do or do not do for us. Their actions help us to decide if we will love them back.

No one is perfect, and it is my belief that an individual should not allow someone to dictate how and when they can love them. There are some who will only love another person based on how the other person treats them. There are some people who will love another person solely because of how that person treats them. I understand that loving someone is not easy, nor is it comfortable. But there is no question that we all must have love to survive.

I believe that the number of homeless people would decrease if more people had love for those individuals, be it family or non-family. Tragically, some suicides occur because those individuals do not feel that they are loved, or they are not loved the way they want to be loved.

Now, let me revisit love being dangerous. There have been fatalities due to one person's *love* for another person. For instance, one person finds out that the person they love most is sharing and giving their love to someone else. Because of this betrayal, several things may occur.

1) Love may turn to anger and anger into violence to the point that a life or lives are lost.

2) One may direct the pain of being cheated on toward himself and begin to abuse drugs and alcohol or even hurt himself to the point of taking their life.

3) Take revenge by hurting the person the way they hurt them or by getting close to someone who is close to that person, like a best friend or family member.

4) Sadly, if children are in the equation, they may take it out on them in ways that may damage the children for a lifetime. THE CHOICE OF LOVE IS EASY!!!

Earlier in this chapter, I mentioned regret, where one may regret giving his or her heart to a person they feel did not deserve it, merely because the relationship did not work out. I am convinced that you should not regret the love you have shared because you may not know how much that love benefited the other person. Furthermore, you may not realize how much that other individual needed your love at that time. They may currently carry that love with them, even though you are no longer in contact.

Regret reflects the past that did not work out in your favor. When we reflect on love, we should have no regrets because we have little, if any, control over the outcome. When a person looks in a mirror, the reflection is their own. Love can be fearful when we experience situations that may be life threatening, physically damaging, or when family members and children are involved. Love and fear can go hand and hand.

For example, how many times has one said she loves someone during sex but later has a fear of letting her partner know she is pregnant? Even worse is the fear of telling someone that he is not the father. Letting a loved one know a child is on the way can go the other way; the guy can get another woman pregnant and have a fear of what will happen when he delivers the news to the woman he loves.

There are some cases where fear can outweigh love, and the truth is taken to the grave. Can you imagine a person being so in love with someone that they do not want to hurt that person because he or she is in fear of what the outcome may be? Perhaps someone regrets what he did and is fearful of telling the truth due to the potential danger that this situation may bring. It happens, and we have little, if any, control over the outcome.

In a sense, we never truly know completely how the next person will react to the situation, as I mentioned earlier. We can only assume or speculate. Past experiences with that loved one may take precedence, such as a violent past, where love has become a fist, an open hand, or an object that inflicts bodily harm. A lot of parents may beat, punish, or chastise their child when he does or says something that he should not. They believe this *tough love* type of discipline will mold their children into better people. Either way, it is done out of love.

In relationships, men and women do the same thing. The law outweighs *certain types* of love. Today, if a man wrongly chooses to show his love physically and hits a woman, the consequences are much more damaging than ever, regardless of if he is married or not.

Moreover, you make a choice to love, and there are so many other people who fall under that umbrella of love.

When children are not biologically yours, they still need to be loved, even if you do not care for the parent(s) of those children. Love must extend in a certain way to ex-spouses or partners because that individual helped create that child. You cannot take out your anger on a child because he or she may look or act like your ex. Love on your child daily, even if the child looks exactly like their mother or father whom you are no longer with or that you hate with a deep passion.

Love must be given to pets, also. Yes, pets. So many people may love their pets more than they love humans, and once they allow you in, your love extends to the pets as well. This may be a problem for some people, along with children who are not biologically theirs. Also, the fact that some individuals remain close friends with their exes for unknown reasons could be problematic, and all those factors could make it harder to love someone. I have heard a saying that *the heart has a mind of its own*. We must understand that these are choices that will lead to consequences when it comes to the CHOICE OF LOVE.

I haven't read the book, but I know the story!! The Choices and Consequences that you make in life can dictate the outcome of your future, be it good or bad. Within a short time, Bo has relived his past until now in this biography of his life.

— KEISA ATKINSON BELOVED SPOUSE

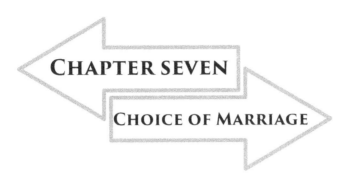

CHAPTER SEVEN

CHOICE OF MARRIAGE

FROM LOVE TO MARRIAGE, normally, that is how it works, or does it? There are many different types of marriages. For instance, in a pre-arranged marriage, two families discuss the gender of their children with the intention of marriage between them. The girl of one family is raised to become the wife of the other family's son. This child does not have a clue that her husband has already been chosen for her before she even knows what marriage is. In this case, love may or may not be involved, but the control that two fathers and a future husband have, like in a prearranged marriage agreement, wanting to keep money, business, or a way of life within the two families. The bride and groom are extremely loyal, not only to each other but even more so to their families, often because of cultural reasons.

A common law marriage is when a state may recognize a couple as legally married, although they have not registered the marriage via paperwork or by a civil or religious ceremony. The couple usually has lived together or been companions for a certain number of years. This may be a situation where two people are involved in a relationship, but for whatever reason, they do not want to legally marry.

Some people are in common-law marriages but may not know it. A common law marriage is when a couple has not formally or religiously registered their marriage but have been in a relationship for a period. If you are unsure about what qualifies as a common-law marriage in your state, you can research the requirements that classify you as being in a legal marriage versus a common-law marriage. This is another good example of choice (living together) and consequence (married under common law).

Another choice that has gained popularity is same-sex marriage, especially since more states have legalized the union. When I was an adolescent growing into a teenager, this was unheard of. That is not to say that same-sex relationships were not happening, but the legalization of it was not. What a choice is made when two people put aside what is looked down upon by society and certain religions to love unconditionally! I am sure that same-sex marriages have problems also, but same-sex couples are divorcing at half the rate of opposite-sex couples. According to data published by the Williams Institute at the UCLA School of Law, in 2011, the divorce rate for same-sex couples was 1.1% per year, while the divorce rate for straight couples was 2% per year.

Some of the problems, I imagine, are centered around having children, how to adopt, how to conceive, foster children, or even having urges or the desire to go back to a traditional relationship between and man and a woman. With this new option, we cannot assume that when someone says they are married that they are married to someone of the opposite sex. As I stated in the beginning, the choice of love may lead to the choice of marriage. The consequences may be wanting to start a family and having to involve a third person to make that happen. I am not saying that these consequences are negative, but they may have some repercussions later in the marriage.

Next, we have the "baby marriage," where a couple gets married because of a pregnancy. There are several factors that I believe go into this decision. For example, a couple decides that it is time to get married since they have been together for so long, and the baby is the deciding factor in making the family complete. Religion may play a role when a couple is influenced or pressured by the pulpit from repeatedly hearing how fornication and shacking up is a sin, and a curse may be put on a couple/family unless they get married and make it right before God. The spiritual pressure leads the couple to marriage.

This may work for some relationships, but for others, it is a factor in the high divorce rate in our society. There are people who were victims of broken homes and do not want that cycle to continue within their families. This may be true of one of the parents or both. There are many individuals who want a much different life for their children than what they had growing up. This, too, can have a positive or negative effect on those who were raised with one parent or raised in the foster care system. Ultimately, they are determined to break the cycle, and in doing so, they get married to keep their family intact.

In certain cases, love may or may not be the foundation for matrimony. I say that because a child can be conceived from a one-night stand, then months later, a wedding takes place. Another scenario is when one or both individuals are in other relationships, but because of their history, they hook up from time to time, and on one of those occasions, a child is the result. They recognize that they cannot stay away from each other physically, and because of the circumstances, they decide to have occasional sex.

Traditional marriage is when two people feel that they have found their soul mate, that special person that they cannot live without, or that person who makes their heart skip a beat each time they hear their voice. This couple may have known each other for over half their lives and cannot or do not want to be with anyone else on earth. Consequently, they 'tie the knot" in holy matrimony.

Online dating is another choice that leads to marriage, where individuals do not have time for a more traditional way to date get to know someone prior to marriage. Social media dating has also taken over, and singles are able to post pictures, personal qualities, thoughts, concerns, and characteristics, along with future aspirations. Therefore, from the posts, comments, and likes, a seed of marriage can be planted and a date set for sooner or later.

How about the choice of marriage for those who are incarcerated short term or long term? There are some people who are considered hopeless romantics and marry inmates for various reasons, death row inmates, those serving life sentences, or 25 to life sentences with no possibility for parole. On the other hand, there are some who are religious and feel that it is their calling or duty to do the right thing in the Lord's eyes.

There are situations where a couple just met, was dating for a short amount of time, or have been together for years. Then the criminal justice system steps in, and one of them must serve a significant amount of time. Prior to the law coming into the picture, this couple had *no plans* to get married and decided to say I do, only because the judge handed down a life sentence. I am not saying that these marriages are destined for divorce, but the consequences may be damaging, and in many cases, they may work out for the best.

Marriage is the toughest choice that requires so much every day. I like to say that it is the toughest thing you will ever have to do in life! I say that because everything else in life, you can just walk away from, like a job, for example. If a job gets too stressful, you can just put your two week notice in and never come back. If there is a change in the front office, and you do not like it, you can walk out without saying a word.

If you are dating for a period, with or without kids involved, and you wake up one morning and say, "I'm done," or "This isn't working," you can just walk out and never return. But if you are married, this is often not the case because once you take that walk down the aisle and take that oath before the Lord, everything changes. Any decisions should be made not only for you but for the benefit of the family financially, professionally, geographically, or anything else that has a direct impact on the marriage.

Now, if one decides that it is too much for whatever reason, you can walk away, but by law, you are still considered legally married. After which, your title will now be considered separated or become estranged husband or wife, while the process of divorce can take years or even longer with children involved. Moreover, when children are involved, it makes it even more difficult to leave the marriage because of the immediate and long-term damage it may cause to everyone.

It is humorous how a marriage license can cost $50, but filing for an average divorce may range anywhere from $500 to $5,000 or more. Because of the costs, instead of paying and finalizing the divorce, many couples remain married, moving forward with living their lives as if they are single, not wearing their wedding ring or acknowledging that they are still legally married.

Marriage is extremely tough, but on the flip side, it can be the most beautiful union on earth when two people wake up with their spouse in mind every day and go to bed with the desire to wake up the following day and make it even better than the day before. When a person prays more for his or her spouse than they do for themselves, life is beautiful. Those good days turn into months, and those months turn into years, and blessings will continue to flow. What one should desire is that the good days outweigh the bad days. If this is the case, then you have a wonderful marriage.

Having a spouse who is a friend, partner, lover, and soul mate is something special. If you are missing a category or two in what it takes to make a marriage work, that only means you have more work to do. Marriage is like pledging a fraternity. The real work begins after you cross the "burning sands" or during the first two years. For those marriages that are fortunate to make it past the honeymoon phase, congratulations!

I have been married multiple times, and I will say that marriage is extremely difficult when you do not have parents who are married or someone close to you who is or has been married. I can only speak for myself, and how difficult it was during the times I was married. I was taught that the husband was/is the provider, and that was it. I did not know many of the other things that went into making my marriage work. There was no blueprint to follow, and I was totally selfish in my marriage. I only wanted what was best for me in my career, regardless of if relocation and uprooting my family was involved.

I was selfish in the bedroom. When I wanted sex, I wanted it even if she was tired from working and then coming home to fulfill her motherly duties with the children. Even if she was sick, I needed my fix, and her health did not matter to me at that time. When I wanted to go out, and she had something to do as well, I was selfish because I felt that it was her responsibility to make sure the kids were taken care of. That was not my job. Even if she wanted to take the kids on a family outing, I was a college basketball coach, and that mattered to me more than spending family time.

What a shame that I didn't realize my way of thinking was wrong until it was too late. There is no question that I can give you story after story about how I messed up my marriages, but I want to encourage those who are currently married to hang in there and take it twenty-four hours at a time. The vows say for better or worse, but personally, I believe marriage is extremely tough when, in my opinion, most married couples cheat or are on the down low.

Some couples choose to attend marriage counseling. I recall premarital sessions when the pastor informed us that there were three main reasons for divorce: finances, lack of communication, and sex. Filing for divorce can be a result of one or all three. But what about those marriages that are secure in all three, or do they only think they are secure? Some couples are required to attend a minimum of three pre-marital sessions prior to getting married, and then the next counseling session is not until problems arise or are insurmountable to the point that they end that which was once holy.

My advice is this, why not have counseling sessions every six months, regardless of whether there are problems on the horizon or not? Counseling sessions can aid in supporting several key areas; finances, fruitful and meaningful communication, and sex without scheduling but spontaneous enough to keep both wanting each other more.

I believe couples cheat because something is missing in that union. Whatever is missing, that person knows it starts with communication because they are not sharing with their mate. Your spouse should know before anyone else when something is bothering you and should want to fill that void by any means necessary. On the other hand, if a spouse has voiced his or her uneasiness, but the other spouse does not acknowledge or properly address the problem, then the situation is out of the hands of the spouse who communicated the issue. It is now in the hands of the Lord, and you continue to love that spouse. More problems arise if that spouse begins to share feelings with someone outside of the house, be it a pastor, family member, friend, or person of interest, but most people already know that.

Trust must be present in every aspect of a marriage. Your spouse must trust you enough to know they are the most important person in your world and that you share everything with them. I have known couples who are unhappy in their marriages and seek happiness elsewhere without the spouse having a clue. There are also those who know their spouse is involved with someone else, and if this is the case, there is truly little trust present, and every word, action, or deed, is looked upon as a lie or an untrustworthy gesture. "I am going to the store, and I will be back shortly," is a lie! "Hey, my coworkers are meeting for happy hour after work." Lie! "Next month, I have to go out of town for some training for my job." Lie! These are just some examples of when no matter what you say, your spouse has it in their mind that you are telling a lie, even if all of it is true. Somewhere along the way, something happened or was said to break that TRUST. Either way, the marriage is polluted.

Knowing that trust has been broken or is no longer there, what can you do? You can only control your response to it, and that is loving your spouse despite their shortcomings and flaws, for better or worse. We are imperfect people in an imperfect world, which means that we are going to make mistakes every day. Some of these shortcomings may or may not have been present prior to getting married, but either way, when you said, "I do" or "I will," you accept those shortcomings and flaws and will do everything in your power to love him/her regardless of the situation.

It is asinine to think that marrying someone will change that person because that person must want to change and do whatever is necessary to do so. Change does not happen because you beat, nag, belittle, curse, or degrade that person. It is a personal choice that is made by that individual. So, if you consider yourself a "PEOPLE CHANGER," then get into politics now because we are in desperate need of change in our society. Otherwise, put your trust in God and not in a man or woman.

When you put your trust in God, trust that God will lead your spouse to do the right thing, say the right thing, and become a better person daily. My heart goes out to people who are in an abusive marriage, be it mental, physical, emotional, and or financial. Some people have been known to abuse finances in a marriage, and that hurts just as much as a punch. When one spouse is out there toiling and slaving to make ends meet, and the other spouse is insensitive to how hard their spouse is working for the family, it can feel like a punch to the gut. I cannot imagine what someone goes through daily when they are subjected to physical abuse within a marriage.

I can recall one time when my aunt baked a cake for my uncle's birthday, and she wanted my cousin and I to sing happy birthday when he came home. When he did not come home until late that evening, my aunt was very disappointed, and they argued. My cousin and I were downstairs listening to the shouting, and then we heard him repeatedly hitting her head against the stairs. We rushed up the stairs to find the cake face down on the floor and him on top of her. He was a fierce and intimidating man. When he saw us, he told us to take our asses back down those stairs before he killed us next. My aunt echoed his demand for us to go back downstairs.

I was a young fella, and I never forgot what I saw. To this day, I know that the cake being thrown on the floor hurt her more than the bruises on her body. I only visited them on various weekends, so this probably went on more often than I knew. In that same marriage, I witnessed my aunt stand up to him by saying that was the last time that he would ever put his hands on her, and if he ever thought about it, she would kill him. When we got older, he went from being intimidating to a "try me" type of guy. My aunt stayed true to her vows from then until now, and I respect and love her to the fullest.

My second family in California was high school sweethearts Joyce and Mercer Lawrence Sr. from Louisiana, who adopted me. I saw their marriage grow in so many ways with only two children, a boy, Mercer Jr., and a girl, Chiyah. They were not always financially secure, and I am sure there were other problems that I was unaware of, but the bottom line is they did not allow those circumstances to break or destroy their bond of marriage.

Mom took ill and had to have care twenty-four hours a day. From my perspective, their marriage grew stronger. Dad was by her side, doing everything from bathing her to changing bed linens, cooking and feeding her, watching television with her, and reading to her with the knowledge that her condition would not change. I witnessed how Dad sacrificed his life for their lives.

They also had to bury my brother, and I know that as parents, burying a child was the most difficult thing they ever had to do. Finding out that one's son or daughter is no longer living, then having to make funeral arrangements and put them in the ground can be devastating as well as damaging not only to a family but to a marriage. I witnessed this union as a model for marriage because they did everything together, worked through their situations, and took me in as if I was their biological son. I never felt anything different when it came to them, while some marriages may experience friction or uneasiness when it involves an outsider. We remain close to this day, and I am so grateful and thankful for the example of this marriage that set the bar for me.

My biological mom did not get married until a few years ago. I am not sure if she had a ceremony or not because I was not there. My grandparents were married for fifty-five years until my grandfather passed away. She went on to glory not long after. The interesting thing about them was that I do not recall them ever living together. He did not live with us, and as a matter of fact, I don't think I had ever been to his place. He would come to visit every two weeks, and once I got older, I realized those visits coincided with his pay periods.

My grandmother never mentioned divorce, even though she knew about his other women. Today, she would be considered stupid. Here is another thought-provoking point: She had two children prior to meeting him and gave him five more. She was a political figurehead over public housing in Detroit's Brewster Projects, a wife, a mother, and a politician. He was unfaithful through all that, but she never wavered when it came to her marriage.

Generations before us remained in their marriages regardless of what was going on and never seriously considered ending their marriages. I believe that during the 1990s, things changed for whatever reason, and people, myself included, felt like they could not deal with or did not want to deal with the situations or circumstances within a marriage any longer. I know for a fact that the problems and situations that present themselves are not new, and back in the day, our ancestors went through the same things, if not worse. They managed, however, to keep their union intact.

In my opinion of the vow 'until death do us part,' the word death does not necessarily mean physical death. A lot of marriages end because of an emotional death or a spiritual death. This death occurs when someone has been through so much that they cannot resurrect their emotional well-being to restore or revive that which is lost or dying. Sometimes, people go through so much spiritually in a marriage that no matter how much church, revival services, or counseling they attend, their spirit for their marriage is deceased. In my eyes, all these circumstances mean 'until death do us part.'

What about those double marriages, better known as bigamy, where men or women are married to one spouse but are also married to another. Sure, this is illegal, but it happens. How can someone be in love with two people? How can someone take the walk down the aisle and the oath, knowing it is extremely difficult just to love one person and add another? This choice is dangerous for some and, in so many ways, painful for others.

I often remind myself that God will not put more on us than we can bear, but who do you bear it for and with? Today, we get married and ask questions afterward, like did I make the right decision, or is it too soon? Can people just be together without the marriage title? Most women desire a wedding to remember, and most men want to give their woman the desires of her heart. The reality is that the wedding is for "Them," the wife, and the honeymoon is for us. Some people go into debt trying to have that dream wedding. Others have that dream wedding, then cannot afford to go on a honeymoon. I sometimes wonder about those dream weddings where couples put so much into them financially, emotionally, and physically, and the wedding lasts longer than the marriage.

I realize that I am saying some things that most people may only think about—either way, it is true. Why not just have a simple ceremony, a festive reception, and a dream honeymoon? Save that money you would spend on having friends and family travel from everywhere to attend, just to give their opinion on your ceremony, such as, it was nice, or it was awful, "Shaunte's wedding was better," or they should have done this or that.

Another reason to conserve money on a wedding is that many people who attend are not there to genuinely support the couple. Some people go to weddings only to be seen or to say they were there. I feel that if you plan to get married, you should focus more on the person you plan to spend the rest of your life with and not the other people in your life. If they love you and are happy for you, then they will understand that a simple ceremony makes more sense, and they will do whatever they can to make it memorable.

If money is not an issue, then go all out. I am speaking to those who have the desire to put more into their marriage than their wedding, beginning with the honeymoon. There are several marriage stories that I could share, including my brother Hamilton's twenty years and counting, and my cousin Howard's twenty-plus years, both of whom I stood next to as their best man. I cannot seem to follow their paths because I have been unable to stay married for more than twenty minutes. There are numerous stories that can be told, but the bottom line is the choice of marriage is a difficult one.

Bo, I know this book has taken you longer than expected, but that's what creating masterpieces is all about. Through all of life's trials and tribulations, you didn't give up. You kept pushing through. I can't wait to read your first book!

Love you, bro!

— LEONARD "L BOOGIE" GANT 7TH GRADE MATH TEACHER SAN FRANCISCO, CA

I've known Bo Bivens for over 25 years. I've seen him coach, I've coached with him, and I've coached against him. We've been to basketball camps together throughout the United States

First, he loves his family. He also enjoys mentoring young adults and is very well-respected in our Detroit community. He's an educator and team player as well as someone who the students and players look up to.

I hold him in high regard, and most of all, he is a good friend.

— LEXA PAGE HIGH SCHOOL BASKETBALL COACH SOUTHWEST DETROIT LEGEND

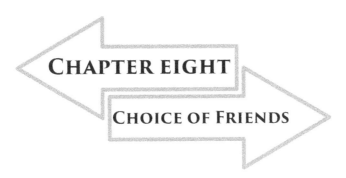

CHAPTER EIGHT

CHOICE OF FRIENDS

How do you choose your friends? Do you choose them based on hobbies or common interests, similar or opposite personalities, because they are your neighbor or a neighborhood affiliation? Do you choose friends due to a shared love of sports or because you work at the same company? Perhaps you inherit your friends based on their lifelong relationship with your family? This is where two FAMILIES are close, and their children grow up together and become close.

Regardless of how, selecting friends is still a choice. You cannot choose your family. When you are born, certain individuals tell you who your family members are, most likely starting with your mother identifying herself and others like your father (possibly), grandmother, grandfather, uncles, aunts, cousins, siblings, and more. You had no choice in the matter, but friends, on the other hand, are a different story. You meet someone, regardless of how you met them, and you open your heart, home, pockets, feelings, and deepest darkest secrets to this person. Why? Because there is something different about that person from all the other people you know. This choice may only happen with a few people.

One's circle of friends is small or should be small. Some people have different categories of friends, homeboy or homegirl, bestie, acquaintance, colleague, teammate, Pat'ner (Los Angeles slang for partner), co-worker, frat brother, sorority sister, business partner, church member, classmate, cellmate, shopping buddy—I do not know them all, but you get the picture.

Men and women choose friends differently. Men choose those with common interests, in most cases, and that is it. We usually do not open up to people easily, nor do we let people into our circle. Once we get a certain level of trust with a few people, then we limit how close anyone else can get. Women can make new friends at the nail shop. Just sitting there getting their nails done, and the person next to them has what they consider a pretty color. She will say ask her what number that is, and the other lady will respond, "Number 28." "I'm going to get that one if it is okay with you?" "Sure, girl, it would look good on you too. "What are you doing tonight?" "Let's get drinks." Now they are best friends.

Men cannot do that. At the barbershop, one guy observes another getting a haircut and comments, "Nice cut. I want a fade like that." When the guy gets out of the chair, he says this cut will look nice on you, too, and then asks him, "What are you doing tonight?" That will never happen. Totally opposite outcomes, but the choice of friends is an especially important life choice.

Some people choose to give their close friends family titles like brother, sister, cousin, auntie, uncle, nephew, niece, pops, moms, and so forth, with no blood or marital attachment. That is big. I cannot speak for everyone, but I know I have done it because I am closer to them than any family member. I grew up with some guys my age, and we went to school together, played ball together, chased the girls together, and broke crimes together. I thought we would be lifelong friends, but I was dead wrong.

It has been said that friends come into your life for a reason and a season. Sometimes you become friends with someone who seems to be born for the purpose of being a friend. When that time is, God only knows. How you will become friends with someone, God only knows. True friendships never end. They may be put on pause for a while, but they never end.

When my family and I moved to Los Angeles, I was blessed to

meet some lifelong friends. I did not plan on it, but it was all God's timing. Ironically, to this day, I cannot stand the West Coast, but living there contributed some invigorating stories and memories to my life's journey. I enrolled in Manuel Arts High School, but I did not want to be on the West Coast, let alone at that school. The only thing that kept me going was basketball.

I did not have one friend at that school, but I did have a friend in the neighborhood, a Hispanic guy named Jose Blanco. That was my guy! He was unlike any other Hispanic guy I had met at that point in my life. He was fearless and could fight. We played ball together, ate together, and his sister, Ovlina, was "muy bonita (beautiful)" or something like that. After school, we would meet and hang out until it was time to go to bed. I cannot remember what school he went to, but I wondered why he did not play for his high school team.

One day, he invited me to sign up with the National Youth Sports Program (NYSP) at the University of Southern California. Naturally, I didn't know what it was or what it was about; I just went because Jose asked me. It was a free sports program that offered enrichment sessions and lunch, just what I needed, plus it was co-ed. Having played sports all my life, I thought the program was fun. I learned how to play soccer and became a better baseball player. The other sports were easy, including swimming.

I was a dog, probably one of the best, if not the best, in the program. During my time there, I befriended Donald Muepo, who was my coach, Zack, his competitive brother, their brother Larry, and sister BB (Astrid). While at Manuel, I did not officially play for the school, but I always worked on my game. A coach watched me work out and asked me to play for his Amateur Athletic Union (AAU) team. James was his name, and the name of the Team was The Los Angeles Tigers. He had us play against teams that were younger to make us look good, but when we played against teams our age, it was much tougher.

We had our nicknames on the back of our jerseys, and there was one guy who had "Hard Time" on the back of his. He was so not hard times to the point that it was funny. He was horrible as far as I was concerned, but Coach James loved him. Then he added this big head, big-lipped guy named Quick. He would get up and down the floor quickly, so I guess that's how he got his name. When he showed up, we typically won those games because he took some of Hard Time's minutes. We had a few other guys that I do not remember, but I took one under my wing named Marcel Capers, who turned out to be rather good. He started at Manuel Arts and went on to do very well at Arizona State.

But getting back to why I did not play at Manuel Arts. I got kicked out for fighting. I still had and have the east side of Detroit in me, and we do not do a lot of talking. However, this guy was unaware of that. One day, when I was minding my business in class, the other students were talking about the guy I fought, who we called Punching Bag. I laughed, and he asked me what I was laughing at, so I pointed to him. He told me to laugh again, and when I did, he said that after school, it would be on. I replied, "After school? We can handle this now in second period."

I started walking toward the door, and when he followed me, I proceeded to whoop his ass. We had a male teacher, and he pulled me off the boy, but as he was pulling me off, I stomped him at least ten times in his face. A lot of what he got in that moment came from me not wanting to be on the West Coast. I took it out on him, and he will never forget the guy that came from Brick City and broke his face.

The consequence was that I had to meet with the principal, who was female, and she called my mom to the school. We were in her office when she told my mom that I had to go because I was the worst student in the school. "No one in this school has ever beat another kid like your son," she said. "He has to go." According to her, when a student is expelled, he is given three choices of schools to transfer to. I was not familiar with any of them. She asked me, and I was mute. My mom said, "Say something." I remember playing ball, and this guy had on a Reseda basketball jersey, and I liked their colors, Carolina blue and navy. The other two came from the principal. If Reseda was full, then the next school on the list would be my next option.

Reseda accepted me, and I had to be bused out to the valley every day, which was about thirty minutes away. I quickly adjusted to the diverse environment, and it did not take long for me to stand out. Being from Detroit, we dressed differently, walked differently, acted differently, and not to mention looked different, especially relative to West Coast people. I would sit alone for nutrition and lunch. Other times, I would take my skills to the court, and that's when I got noticed even more.

There was a tall 6'4", long, lanky, light-skinned kid who was always on the school court, but he did not play for them. When I was younger, it always bothered me when guys had talent but did not play for the school. In any case, Rodney Griggs and I connected on the court, and our relationship extended off the court. He invited me to stay at his home from time to time, as well as attend his church youth ministry program. We did a lot together that I will discuss more later. I played basketball but still only hung with one person until I met this chunky, fat cheeks and braces guy with his name on his white Lakers starter jacket named Mercer Jr.

Mercer was a comedian in every sense of the word. He was a grade behind me, but he had no respect of persons when it came to talking about people. Mercer made you either feel bad, made you laugh, or both. I am laughing while writing this because not a day went by that he did not put a smile on someone's face. He was not an athlete, but you couldn't tell him that. If you did, he would find something to say about you. He had a best friend named Carlton who lived nearby. They hung out and rode the bus together. Carlton was a big, overweight, bowlegged athlete. He could play any sport and was damn good at it all. He was a star baseball player for the school. Because Mercer and Carlton were so close, Carlton and I became close too. Our friend Rodney was the other addition to the crew.

My friendship with Jose remained solid during the summers of

NYSP. Unbeknownst to me, Jamie Hamilton, aka Quick, was also a participant at NYSP and had been for years. He knew Jose as well from participating in the sports program. Quick had an older sister who was a counselor in the program, and she hated Zack Muepo, one of my friends and mentor. They hated each other so much that she gave him three kids and thirty-plus years of marriage and counting.

Quick, who I gave the name J-Rock, and I became the best of brothers and still are to this day. We both went from being participants to becoming JCs (junior counselors) to counselors putting in at least ten years, if not more. Donald and I became close due to our coach and player relationship as I developed into a college basketball player. My Reseda High School crew set us apart from a lot of other crews, not only because of our various styles of dress but also due to the bond we built.

One night at Rodney, aka Pooh's crib, we decided that we would not allow anything to come between our friendship. No woman, no money, or no material thing would drive a wedge through our bond. We decided to create a name for our crew and call ourselves the BV Crew. Rodney chose his name from Pooh Richardson, a point guard at UCLA, and added Baby to it. Carlton became known as Beanni because of this beautiful girl he was attracted to named Monique. She told him his head looked like a bean with a hat on it, so that stuck. Mercer used his name and added Baby Slow. Then we got our neckline cut in the shape of the letter V, which was the creation of the BV Crew; Bo, Baby Pooh, Beanni, and Baby Slow. Later, I adopted the name Slow-Motion from moving and doing everything slowly, and Mercer took on the name Slow-Motion II, or Slow II.

Our friendship was tested time and time again but stood true through and through. There was one situation when I was dating my first West Coast girlfriend, Neda, at Reseda High School. She was cool, and she became cool with the crew. She and I had no issues except when I stayed in the valley for the summer. She felt that I was being untrue and that I was doing whatever I wanted while we were still going together. When I returned home, Neda, Pooh, and her best friend Kathy called me on three-way and informed me that they were an item, and she wanted all the things back that she had given to me, like stuffed animals, jewelry, and more. I was okay with it but somewhat shocked that he would do something like that.

We all shared one locker at school, so the next day, when we all met up there, I could tell Pooh and the crew were extremely nervous about what might happen. When I saw the fear in his eyes, I did not want to cave his chest in any worse than it already was. I reiterated to him that our friendship was intact and that no woman would ever come between us. Ironically, their romance did not last long, and she began to date this Gangsta Crip, who would walk the halls with his crew and look at us sideways. The couple would walk the halls holding hands, which we never did, and look at me like I was small. How funny!

One day when I was on the court, Neda's new boyfriend approached me with his crew and said I better stop looking at his woman or else. By that time, I was established as a student athlete in football, basketball, and track. Plus, I did not want to get expelled again. My crew asked me what happened and what was said. Mercer wanted me to put these hands on him, just because. Later that week, we were walking toward each other down the hall, my ex, her new beau, his crew, and my crew. When we met face-to-face, I told him in front of her that I did not want her. I said I had that already and would never fight over a girl. I went on to tell him, "If you have a problem with me, then we can handle this now. If not, stop looking at me like you want to do something."

After that encounter, we were good. But he was not good with Slow! Slow wanted me to slap the taste out of his mouth, and naturally, that made me laugh. There were many occasions when Slow would cap, or in other words, crack jokes about someone, and they would get upset to the point that they wanted to fight. I would never let anyone touch him. One thing for certain is that I would put these hands on anyone for my crew, and they knew that.

Most people would say that Pooh was wrong for doing what he

did, and our friendship should have ended then. Well, not so. He will forever be my friend/brother because true friendships are extremely hard to come by, not to mention, men do not open themselves up to other men that often. He is my guy for the simple fact that we have been through so much. Our friendship/brotherhood grew even stronger from that situation, and she was only temporary. I have stories about each of the guys in my crew.

One day when Slow and I were walking to the bus stop, I was wearing a pair of classic white with green stripes K-Swiss. Three thugs approached us and asked where we were from. There was one with a cane who said, "Give me those shoes, or I will shoot you." I had already sized them up, and they were clearly out of their league, challenging me. One of them asked the other to hold his bag.

Slow took off running, and I grabbed the guy with the cane. He proceeded to try to hit me with the cane, but I was too strong for him, and I slung him to the ground. While I had him pinned down, the other two took off my shoes. I was not sure if they were going to get some more guys, so I swung on dude while he was down, hit him upside his head, and proceeded back to the crib.

Slow came to my house a while later and asked where they had gone. I responded, "You ran." He told me that he had gone to find a weapon. I told him that all I had were my hands, and that was all we needed. I was upset at Slow for leaving me in that situation and at myself for letting ole boy run away with my shoes. Ironically, after that situation, our friendship/brotherhood grew even stronger. I shared with him that I would have never left him like that, and I would always be there for him, no matter what. Slow had a big heart, and he was always real, not only to me but to everyone. A circle of friends should have at least one person who keeps it real, no matter who was involved in a situation or the issue. For my circle, there was no question that Mercer " Slow Motion II" Lawrence Jr. was *that* friend.

Beanni and I did everything together, from walking into movie theaters and not paying to playing hoops from one court to another all day. From going skating to picking up girls, you name it, we did it —my brother from another mother. But the thing that stood out to me most was the fact that he knew he wanted to play professional baseball. He worked on his game daily and studied hard. He attended games, and the game became a part of him. I, on the other hand, only liked baseball because of him. The support that we gave each other was second to none. He would always encourage and challenge me to be better than anyone I encountered. He was arguably the best athlete in the crew because of his size, and there was no one his age or size who could play any sport better than him. There were probably older guys who were just as good, but pound for pound, he was better.

We did pretty much everything together almost every day. I still do not know how it came to fruition. I did not go to my prom, nor did I have any desire to pay for a ticket, get dressed up, eat food that I did not like, and sit around waiting to take pictures with a lot of people that I saw every day but didn't really care for. After I graduated from high school, he transferred to and became a baseball star at one of the West Coast's most recognized schools, Crenshaw High, home of the Cougars and Rollin' 60s.

Beanni started dating a girl who was cool, but her best friend did not have a date for the prom, and of course, he asked me to take her. My feelings about the prom had not changed, but because he asked me, and because I knew he would do it for me, I agreed on one condition: that I could wear my white with black striped Ice Man Nike tennis shoes. I knew that would change the game, and lord knows I was born to be different. After talking with her, she agreed, so I went.

We rented a limo service, picked them up, met the parents, and headed out. When I pulled out my Ice Man Nikes, my date stated, "I know you are not wearing those to my prom!" When I replied yes and reminded her that we had made an agreement, she said, "I thought that you were playing." I was furious because I felt like I was doing her a favor, and all I asked was to wear my Ice Man Nikes. She said, "I don't want those in my picture."

I looked at Beanni, and he knew the night was going to be ugly. I went into the prom noticeably agitated and mad that this unattractive, ungrateful female had reneged on our agreement. I honestly wanted to leave because I never wanted to go in the first place. She had the nerve to act bold in the limo, and she was a girl that I would have never looked at twice if it wasn't for Beanni.

As the night went on, things got worse. I did not want to dance, so I didn't. I did not want to take pictures, so I did not smile. I'm not sure if I ate anything, either. After the prom, the four of us went to a hotel. Beanni and his girl went inside, but my date and I stayed in the car. I did not hit it either. As a matter of fact, I did not touch her at all. I may have acted a little extreme, but that was how I felt. She should have thought about her actions since I made compromises for her. At any rate, I couldn't wait for Beanni to get done, so we could go, and I never had to see her again.

I apologize for the rant because I know this is about friendship, and I am talking about a horrible experience that I never really wanted to remember. I guess you can look at it several ways, Beanni's girl was looking out for *her* friend, and Beanni knew I would not let him down as a friend, but it only worked out for the three of them. Was I selfish? Nah, definitely not.

Friendships can be life-changing, as in our case. After I graduated high school, I knew I wanted to play college basketball, but I wanted to return home to Detroit and play at the University of Michigan. It is true that they did not recruit me, nor did they have any idea who I was, but I knew I was good enough to play at that level, and that is where I wanted to go.

I enrolled at Santa Monica College (SMC), but prior to that, I was at El Camino College but only stayed there for two days because it reminded me too much of high school. While at Santa Monica College, I worked three jobs just to earn enough money to get back to the Midwest, be closer to my grandmother, and play for Big Blue (University of Michigan). Job number one was as a valet parking attendant when I did not even know how to drive a stick shift. In job two, I bagged groceries at Ralph's Super Market, and at job three, I was a security escort at Santa Monica College while taking classes every day.

I did speak to the Hall of Fame coach, John McMullen, about playing. He asked me to enroll in his basketball class, and boy did I. I became the best player there. My name became "Detroit," and I was known throughout the campus. Coach told me he loved my game, and the following year, it would be my team. He had an abundance of sophomores, and once they had moved on, he would build a team around me.

Junior college, for me, was all about basketball, nothing else. I recall my schedule being art appreciation, music appreciation, beginning basketball, and advanced basketball (only for the players on the team and very educational). While there, I played every day and continued to get better to the point that some of the players wanted me to play on the team immediately.

At that time, Beanni had accepted a baseball scholarship to Grambling State University. All I knew about Grambling was that they had a black football coach named Eddie G. Robinson, nothing else. I was happy for Beanni and wished him nothing but the best. We talked regularly, and he enjoyed being there. At that point, I did not know when we would see each other again. He was doing his thing, and I was doing mine, until one day, when I was walking to one of my very intense learning classes, and Beanni called me. He told me he had attended a Grambling State basketball game the night before. He said, "You can play here because these guys are not as good as you."

That phone call changed my life because I followed up on what Beanni said and called GSU. I spoke to a coach named Rusty Ponton, and he told me that if I transferred from a junior college, I would have to sit out a year of residency. That day, I went into our admissions office and asked the guy behind the desk what I needed to do to transfer to Grambling State University. He got excited because he was from the south and he was the cousin of NBA player Orlando

Woodridge. He submitted the paperwork for me and said I should receive something in the mail very soon.

The next day, I went into the basketball office to speak to Coach John McMullen and informed him of my dilemma. He poured his heart out to me and said he would hate to lose me, and he was so looking forward to coaching me, but Grambling State was Division I, and the number one goal of all players, once they enrolled in junior college, was to play in Division I. He also told me that he knew I would do well because he'd witnessed my body of work.

To this day, I have nothing but the utmost respect for Coach McMullen for not only believing in me but reinforcing the confidence that was already present, not to mention giving me an opportunity to show what I was capable of. A few weeks later, I got a letter from Grambling State University, accepting me as a transfer student, all because a friend not only knew me but also loved me enough to make a call to let me know how he felt about me as a player. The rest is history. Some friends do not want to put you on their shoulders to elevate you, if or when they can, because you may outshine them, or they will just let you do it on your own and may not help at all.

I mentioned J-Rock earlier, but I think he would say the same thing about my phone call to him. He was playing at Columbia College for the Claim Jumpers in Stockton, California. I wasn't sure about his plans, but I saw in him what Beanni saw in me—that our body of work was greater than what I witnessed around me. J-Rock and I would work on our game for countless hours a day, and we did not need to play five-on-five. We would play one-on-one until it was too dark for us to see the basket. Neither of us wanted to lose, nor did we ever concede to each other. It was the best competition I ever had, including all the pros that I played against.

We were like Cain and O-Dawg from the movie *Menace II Society*. You did not want to see us together. I probably was Cain, and he was O-Dawg. J-Rock did not give a fuck who, what, when, or where we played. We would play anywhere and against anyone, and this was during a time when gang violence was at its peak, which meant some people would not play in certain hoods because they were afraid, but not us. If we even thought they were playing somewhere, or if we heard that the ballers would be playing at a certain location, we went. When we left, they knew we were the best duo backcourt regardless of who showed up.

I recall us playing an extremely physical game in one gym, physical to the point that when this one guy went up to the hoop, Rock knocked him down. This guy was very hostile when he got up and came at Rock. I remember Rock two-piecing him like Mike Tyson. Rock said to him, "Just let me know if you want some more." Once again, we were not in our hood, and his boys were all in the gym. No one else made a move, then Rock said, "Now, we can ball, or we can fight. It's up to y'all." I was the one who stayed ready but did not talk. The look I gave said enough. They decided that neither was the best alternative, and that was the last game.

J-Rock and I would have our heated one-on-one battles but would hug, kiss, and go eat afterward. That is almost unheard of today, with guys being extra sensitive about having too much estrogen between them. Our friendship was deeper than most, and I knew we were alike in so many ways. We both were full of aspiration and determination and had a tremendous work ethic that was growing daily. I recall a conversation when we talked about his season coming to an end and him not having any scholarship offers but still having the desire to play Division I basketball. In the words of Beanni, "You can come play here. These guys are not as good as you are," and the rest is history. Rock came, and the three of us became roommates. Our love and friendship grew even stronger. Oh, I forgot, "Baby Boy" James Vendergrift roomed with us also.

Picture this, three awesome athletes and one unbelievable mascot under one roof. It was something out of a script. Rock and I were the guys on the hardwood, Beanni was the man on the diamond, and Baby Boy was the tiger amongst all tiger mascots. We supported each other all the time, and I think Baby Boy enjoyed being our roommate even more because he would use that to get women to come over. He would say, "Bo Bivens is my roommate," or "Jamie Hamilton is my roommate," or "That guy who just hit that home run is my roommate," not that he was our roommate, but that we were his roommate.

He got more women just by being our roommate than most guys who were better looking or more well-known, to the point that we thought it was the best foreplay move ever. These girls would already be over when we came in, and they would say, "He told me that you live here, but I didn't believe him. Now I do," smiling and wet. Then Baby Boy would have a smile on his face and say, "Yeah, Bo," while walking into the room. Friendship is a choice because every person you meet will not be your friend.

I do have to let you know about my first college roommate, Sterling Black. I mentioned earlier that I went to Grambling State University with a small bag, my basketball, and nothing else. When I walked into Pinchback Hall, room 418, my roommate had everything, sheets, comforter, pillow, refrigerator, TV, microwave with food and snacks, all the things a poor broke college student wished for. We hit it off from the start. S-Dog was from Southfield and played basketball for the Southfield Blue Jays. The boy was a flat-out shooter with a smooth left-handed stroke that you could not leave open. The seed for our friendship was planted on day one, and we are still close to this day. I love him also as a brother.

I must share a few stories about my roommate, who I affectionately call "S." I still say that when he arrived at Grambling, he was a virgin, but he argues me down in denial. Ironically, his first girlfriend at Grambling State is the cousin of my ex-wife. She turned my guy S completely out! She did things to him that he had only seen in pornos. She, too, was from the east side. He would come to the room, complaining that she wanted it too much. And if she called, he told us to say he was not there, so he could recuperate. How funny is that! He did get his share of coochie after that because she opened him up and elevated his confidence. He made me proud, and we have numerous stories to share.

Our friendship is much more than sex stories, though. Our families are remarkably close to the point that our children know and love each other, and he always has his door open to me. I am not sure how many college roommates, male or female, are still close more than twenty years later, but to me, that is a sign of true friendship.

I can honestly say that in college, I met a lot of people and made a lot of friends, but I only have a few true friends. John Joubert, aka Smooth, is one of those true friends, and we were brought together by one of his close friends, Carl Ramsey. Both were from Southwest Detroit. I give Carl credit for assembling the greatest one-year intramural basketball team ever at Grambling State University called The Bad Boys. He saw me shooting on an outside court behind Drew Hall by myself and asked if I wanted to play for his team. I did not know anyone, and I wanted to play, so I said yes. Once he found out that I was from the east side of Detroit, he said that our team would be called The Bad Boys.

He got a bunch of guys from various parts of Michigan, including Detroit, Flint, Southfield, Southwest, one from Lansing, and one from Chicago. Oh, I can't forget Rance from California. We jelled together from the start, and most of the guys remain close to this day. My backcourt mate, Keith "Patches" Lamont Bowmen, and I are the closest. I almost forgot to say that Baby Boy was a member of our championship team, also. Carl got in some trouble with the university and was suspended for the entire year, but every chance he got, he would say that my boys from Southwest Detroit, Nice and Smooth, were coming. I had heard about Smooth prior to him coming but did not expect our friendship to be where it is today.

The Bad Boys played in the Turkey Tourney, a Thanksgiving tournament held in the fall semester for intramural teams. The tournament was sponsored by none other than Sweet Lou Collins, who I like to say put me on the map at GSU because, prior to that tournament, no one truly knew who I was. After stealing the ball from some bum and dunking on his head, I walked away with the MVP trophy, and word got around. Thanks again goes to Carl Ramsey and Sweet

Lou. The Bad Boys ended up coming in second in the intramural championship. Losing at the buzzer in front of the largest crowd ever for an intramural basketball game.

One of my favorite G-Men (Grambling State University athletes), Willie "Jake" Reed, played on that team, but he went on to play professional football as a wide receiver with Chris Carter and Randy Moss for the Minnesota Vikings. Andrew "Poncho" Glover was my starting center on GSU's hoop squad, and he played tight end for the Vikings as well.

After my introductory season of intramural basketball, I earned a spot as one of the Elite 12 G-Men on the basketball team. Smooth came that next semester, and we hit it off just like his name. He and Nice were like twins because when you saw one, you saw the other. They dressed alike, walked alike, and played every intramural sport at Grambling State, including softball, because baseball was their thing in Southwest Detroit. Smooth was eager to play for the G-Men, but he, too, had to sit out with his 6'4" long frame.

Carl Ramsey returned and created another team called Just Do It. This term is trademarked by Nike. They were solid, talked a lot of trash, and were always ready to fight. At that time, I coached two teams that I had put together, Hardcore Ballers and Crowd Pleasers, and I also coached Just Do It. No one could beat my teams.

While coaching intramurals, I recruited a guy that I saw play, who I had to have on one of my teams. His name was Sababu "Boo" Meeks. He had broad shoulders and a strong game to go with them. Boo was arguably the best player that never played for the university. He was a rebounding machine from Chicago by way of Oklahoma City (OKC) who could dunk on anybody. He fit right in with the expectations of the squad and with his teammates. Boo had a sense of humor like no other, and the fact that he hated to lose drew us even closer together. Hard Core Ballers was the first team in GSU history to win the state intramural championship, and we could not have done it without him. Our friendship extended beyond basketball, and there was no question that it was for life.

Whenever I was in Chicago, I stayed at Boo's place, and we would have real conversations and memorable experiences. He would visit when I was coaching at Western Michigan University. While his sister was his only sibling, he told everyone that I was his brother. We experienced a lot together and shared everything, with the exception of the fraternity that he chose. I am a member of Omega Psi Phi, and he is a member of Kappa Alpha Psi, both founded in 1911.

I recall going to Chicago and meeting his father for the first time. That is where he showed me his new toy, a white Suzuki bike, and he told me that he was waiting for a white helmet and white jacket to go with it. For some reason, I got nervous just looking at the bike, but he was too excited for me not to be excited for him. Unfortunately, that bike ended our friendship.

Boo was riding his bike home one rainy night after working his job with the railroad when the driver of an 18-wheeler beside him tried to switch lanes. The wet road caused the trucker to slide and hit him. Boo survived the accident. When I went to see him in the hospital, he was in a vegetative state, but he responded to my voice. Tears rolled down his face. I knew I had to be strong for him, but it was killing me to see him like that. I broke down when I left, and unfortunately, that was the last time I saw him alive. Rest in peace, my friend/my brother Boo. The other interesting thing is that I found out this information from our mutual friend Tanisha who worked with Boo at the University of Illinois-Chicago. I met her through him, and we became close friends.

Smooth and I were criminal justice majors, and we both had an interest in a particular Greek organization, so we became close. I mentioned before that the Southwest Boys played every sport, but Smooth never played for the G-Men. Carl Ramsey begged Smooth to play football, and Smooth could not let the guy down who got him to Grambling State, so he decided to play, and play he did. He looked like Calvin Johnson out there until he stepped into a sprinkler hole and twisted his knee. He cried like the city of Brooklyn when Biggie passed away, and I sincerely felt bad for him because I knew how much he wanted to play for Da G!

After rehabbing for serval months, it became more difficult for him to return to his division I potential. Though we were never teammates, our Detroit ties kept us close to the point that he was my first official bald fade haircut client. It was not the best cut, and I thank God his hair grew back. We also had the same aspiration to obtain criminal justice degrees, and we both attended weekly meetings on visits to Angola State Penitentiary.

As the days turned into weeks, and those weeks turned into years, Smooth was responsible for one of the best days of my life by asking me to be the godfather of his unborn child. I am not sure how other guys feel about being asked to take on this responsibility given from one friend to another, but to me, there is no greater honor than for a man to be asked to become the person his friend entrusts his child to if something were to happen to him. I am emotional right now thinking of how our friendship became a lifelong commitment of trust and love. This can also hold true for a woman being asked to be a godmother by a friend.

I did not know how selecting godparents worked. I was married when Smooth asked me, and my wife felt a way about not being asked to be the godmother. I was always under the impression that when the husband is asked to become the godfather, then the wife is automatically considered the godmother, especially since the child would spend so much time around the couple. I have learned this is not always the case. All I know is that my friend, my brother, loved me enough to anoint me as the godfather of Diarra Joubert. What a blessing. I love her because my friend loved me enough to cement our friendship until I have no more breath in me. Friendship is a choice that has major consequences in life.

I could not end this topic without asking this question; Can people of the opposite sex be close friends without being intimate or after being intimate? This is one of those discussion topics that could go either way. I say yes and no. Here is why I say it can be both.

When two individuals of the opposite sex start a friendship, they have some type of attraction to each other, whether it is physical, based on intellect, shared artistic interest, or their families are close and do a lot of things together. Some people have a mutual friend who introduces the two, and they become close afterward. I know that there are many ways to become friends that I may have failed to mention, but you get the picture. I have a few of my own to share.

While at Grambling State University, I became close friends with a young lady from my hometown, and we both matriculated in the same field of study. We also were regularly active in various clubs on campus. By seeing one another so much, and our personalities meshing so well, we became closer. Studying together and challenging one another to know the material are some of the reasons we became so close. I always got the better grades. One of the clubs that we were involved in was Criminal Justice Club. I was Mr. Criminal Justice, and she was Ms. Criminal Justice, and we were also members of the Michigan Club. The Michigan Club would participate in joint activities with the Windy City Club, including cookouts.

On one occasion, I was extremely tired from the 5:00 a.m. practice that morning, and she was tired from Army ROTC physical training, so we both got into bed to nap at about the same time. Some people may not believe this, but I never looked at her as anything more than a friend. For me, there was absolutely no attraction whatsoever. Therefore, nothing happened that day.

She dated one of my teammates on the GSU men's basketball team. He was a known hoe, but he called himself a mack. This guy knew we were close, and he would come into the locker room, bragging about who he had been with the night before, testing me to see if I would tell her. I never did. She would ask me if he was cheating on her, but I always removed myself from the situation. It was not my place to tell, even though she was my best friend. Plus, I did not have any concrete proof. For all I knew, they both could have been testing me to see if I was a loyal friend or loyal teammate. If he was cheating, she would have to find out on her own.

One night she called and asked if I would take her over to his place for the specific purpose of finding proof of his infidelity. I drove her there as any true friend would. When she went into his home, she found out that her intuition was correct because some broad was there. My friend and my teammate talked, then they kissed, and she and I left with me shaking my head. She said, "Don't say nothing, Bo." I laughed, and we drove off.

We talked about everything, and we talked daily, but we never crossed the line. I always had a girlfriend or woman that I entertained but would never label as my girlfriend, and she was always in a relationship, so that was the extent of it. Friendship was a choice in this matter. But one day, after both of us had broken up with our respective mates, she asked, "Why don't we get together?"

I was uncertain, but she explained that we had been friends for a long time and knew so much about each other, so why not give us a try? I kept thinking of how much I had never truly looked at her like that before, but on the flip side, how much fun we had when we were together and how supportive she had been since we met. I thought, *Why not? What the hell?* In this case, my female friend became my wife and the mother of my kids. What a friendship, and we are still FRIENDS today.

During this time, I had another female friend who was older. I believe she was a junior when I first got to Grambling State. She was an Orchesis, the name of GSU's dance team, so they would practice in the women's gymnasium on the stage while I would be on the court, working on my game. Her name was Janeen Griffin, and she was from Chi-Town. We would talk about life at Da G. She truly helped me with my transition and adaptation to a small country town, not to mention the women.

Neen, as I called her, would tell me who was off limits or no good for me and about the ones who would share their wet dreams about me with her. I learned so much from her, and I am sure she learned other things about me as well. Our friendship never crossed the line, and I know many people will not understand how a male and female could remain friends without anything sexual or intimate between them. My girl at the time would always wonder if there was something going on between us and why we spent so much time together. One big question I have is if two friends start relationships, and their partners want them to end their friendships with the opposite sex, should they end them, keeping in mind that they were friends before they got into the relationship?

But back to Neen. Because of our friendship, a phone call changed my life. I will never forget lying on the couch in LA during April of 2003 when my phone rang, and it was her. She asked me if I wanted to go on the Fantastic Voyage, better known as the Tom Joyner Cruise. I said, "Sure, how much do I have to pay?" Her reply was, "Nothing. I just need you to run the basketball tournament for me." My reply was, "No Doubt." Because of our friendship, for the last seventeen years, I have worked on the cruise and met so many influential people from various parts of the world.

One person is Warren "Dub" Baker. He and I worked together on the basketball tournament. The southeast native who attended University on the Hill, Prairie View A&M, pledged Kappa Alpha Psi fraternity because of Neen, and we are still very tight seventeen years later. He is not the only one. Shout out to Candice & Kyle and the entire events team, not to mention my dawg Flatbread "TA" Indy!! My "Last Dawg in the Pound" Lance Guess, I love you, big fella. Another Dawg that I consider a true friend is Larry King from North Carolina A&T, where they are known as GHOE (Greatest Homecoming on Earth).

Catking and I met on the cruise sixteen years ago at the Famous Beach Party, and we have been connected ever since. Our friendship over the years has grown in many ways. He is quick to let me know when I am wrong, and he will give me the truth regardless of the situation. He is also the biggest court jester I know. He loves to be the life of the party and make sure everyone else has a great time. He makes GHOE what it is in my eyes. He and his line brothers are the only reason I ever attended GHOE and have only missed once in the last four years.

Larry will frequently call to check in on me and the family, and our friendship remains intact today. There is no doubt in my mind that I would have never had the opportunity to meet the individuals that I have if it had not been for the friendship that Neen and I share. What is deep to me is that I am sure she passed up a lot of other numbers and names that she could have asked, but she chose me. We are still extremely close to this day without ever having crossed the line.

Speaking of University on the Hill, PVU, there was a guy who played for Prairie View a few years prior to me but began coaching while I was playing. After playing, I began coaching as a graduate assistant. He was still coaching when we connected at that time. His name is Leonard Gant, and I affectionately call him "LG." Ironically, he is a Nupe (Kappa Alpha Psi Member) also. I never knew his college sweetheart, and he never knew mine. We talked basketball and those "God's Gifts" around us.

After I graduated with my Bachelor of Science in criminal justice, I moved to Fort Hood, Texas, and got married. While in Fort Hood, which is a military town, we were volunteering during a Juneteenth celebration, and who was there? None other than LG and his wife. She was an officer in the military like my wife at the time. He nor I had any affiliation with the military except for our wives, but we were two guys from two different places who played ball in the Southwestern Athletic Conference and ended up in a town only because of the people we were married to.

Our friendship grew even stronger from that celebration. We have remained close as brothers to the point that I call his two kids, Lauren and Leonard, my niece and nephew. He has helped me in many ways by giving me advice about marriage, my career, or just about life in general. My relationship with him is another great choice of friendship.

There was another guy that I met while we both were college

assistant coaches. His name is Rondre Jackson, and we exchanged business cards at a recruiting event out west. Our friendship began in the 1990s, and we are still in contact to this day. He later moved up to coaching with the Los Angeles Sparks and called me to work the draft camp, which I did for a few years. This is one of those rare relationships/friendships where it takes two to remain true to each other. He always sends holiday texts and birthday wishes, which lets me know I am on his mind and a friend.

I will never forget two specific calls that I received from him. One was when he got let go from the Sparks, and we talked for a few hours. The second was when he was hired by the Los Angeles Lakers, and we talked for a few hours. He asked me to work with him during the summer, which I did for nine years, or should I say, until they had a change in the front office. We talked after the notice was handed down, and we remained in constant contact. I know there is someone reading this who has encountered a lifelong friend in a similar way. Rondre and I have that special bond that takes two to sustain and be meaningful. I love you, Big Fella, and appreciate you more than you know. Keep reaching for the stars, and let me know when you need me to grab a few for you.

Have you ever hit it off with someone over the phone, and that person turns out to be a godsend? Well, I have, and this guy became close during a valley period of my life. A new administration transitioned into an institution where I was coaching, and they let us go. I was out of a job with a family, and one of my former players talked to this stranger about an opening at his college. We spoke over the phone, and the connection was made between Athletic Director Keith McKinnon and me. The interview was set, and afterward, he offered me the position of head coach and assistant director of athletics. From that day forward, we became Batman and Robin.

When Keith left that program to move to another, he took me with him. After that, we became closer, and I had more titles to put on my resume, along with experience that I may not have gotten anywhere else. Because of how close we became, I asked him to be the godfather of my youngest son. He welcomed the opportunity and has upheld his obligation like none other. I do not know what I would have done without him during my time of tribulation. Unfortunately, because of the mother of my son, Keith and I have not spoken in years.

You have read that my guys and I said we would never let any woman come between our friendship. Well, he did not get that memo because he has not reached out due to her bitterness toward me. As for me, I tried, but any relationship takes two to do their part to build, sustain, or strengthen it. I love big dawg and everything he has done, is doing, and stands for, but when you know someone longer than another person, I just believe the length of time and love should mean more. I consider myself a true and loyal friend, a choice I made a long time ago.

Another story of friendship took place when I was getting my master's degree at Grambling State University. I befriended a woman I met in the intramural center when she was a freshman. She was from Chicago and attended a school outside the city, R. Thornridge High School in Dalton, IL, to be exact. She always wore red shorts and a blue shirt, her high school colors. I am not sure how many pairs of each she had, but she wore them daily. Her name was Sheron Wright, and we hit it off from the first jumper I watched her make in the gym. She was a bit on the heavy side at the time but always had high self-esteem, which is a character trait that I admire most.

Needless to say, she became not only a friend but my little sister. From her high school boyfriend, who is now her husband, to my two nephews, Jaquon and Rianne, and everything in between, we share it all. Some have speculated that there was something more than a beloved friendship, even her husband. What we have, very few will understand or have in a lifetime. Even now that she has removed the weight and made a commitment to keep it off, I have never looked at her in any other way than my little sis. She has demonstrated an unwavering love for my family and me since the day we met. I could not have asked for a better friend/sister in my life. In case you are wondering, we have never crossed the line.

Let me touch on some cases that may have or will arise in one's lifetime. With male/female friendships, for example, you have those friendships that may have begun due to a physical attraction that evolved into a relationship, but after some time, the couple frequently argued, and the relationship became toxic to the point that it was not healthy, so they made the choice to become only friends again. They realized that the decision to remain friends was more beneficial. They often talk and continue to sustain their friendship with or without crossing the line again. Another case would be when two people start out as friends, their friendship grows stronger over the years, and they decide to take their relationship to another level. They have that one night of ecstasy but regret it afterward. That would be the first and last time, and afterward, they decide to just be friends, nothing more. They made the choice of friendship.

My last question about friendship is this: what do you do when your spouse or significant other asks you not to be friends any longer with the person you consider a lifelong friend, especially when that friendship may last much longer than the relationship, engagement, or marriage you are in? Do you end the friendship as asked or demanded? Or do you secretly remain friends? Some have ended life-long friendships, and others have done the latter. Either one can be incredibly stressful, not to mention damaging to a relationship or marriage.

There are some opposite-sex friendships that help the current relationship by giving advice or stepping in as an advocate for their friend, even to the point that one of them may be dealing with an issue, let's say, a *lack of sexual satisfaction* and that friend helps them to *relieve the stress,* but never says a word to anyone. True friends will always be true friends. I know it is not right on either part, but I also know that some mindsets are 'I won't tell if you don't' or 'No one has to know.' The most common is, 'Keep this between us,' and they go on living their lives by remaining close friends.

Understand that close friends are not only there physically but financially, spiritually, emotionally, and in any other way there is. These choices of friendship are sustained by trust, love, and a bond that is unbreakable regardless of what others say. Only those individuals know how strong their friendship will forever be.

Friendship is a choice that has major consequences in life. My closest and best friend is my son Zeek. Son, I could not have prayed for a better friend to be my son. I share everything with you because I want you to be better. I give you everything because I do not want you to want for anything. I do not want you to make the mistakes, choices with negative consequences, that I have made. I want you to be a better man than I am. When that time comes, I want you to be a better father than I am, and I want you to be a better brother than I am. God has Jesus as his son, and everyone, Christians and non-Christians, talk so much about what he has meant to their lives, but God gave me you, and you mean more to me than anything as my son and my friend.

"Like minded and scholarly attainment brought us together, but our bond of friendship has kept us together. Bo has always been a true brother to me, and working with him was an unforgettable experience. I wish you nothing but the best that God has to offer you. This is just the beginning. See it through."

— MIKE STEWARD BRIDGE BUILDER PROGRAM,
FOUNDER ORANGE, FL

CHAPTER NINE

CHOICE WORDS OF THANKS

I KNOW there are several stories and individuals that I have failed to mention, but they are not forgotten. I want to thank those individuals from the east side of Detroit who took time out to give me the survival tips that I needed to make it out. I want to thank those grade school teachers at Foster Elementary who went beyond what was required and taught from their hearts to help me become a better reader, writer, and overall student.

To my teachers at Pelham Middle School who recognized my potential early, I want to thank you also. To everyone at Murray-Wright High School, from teachers to coaches, and custodians, much love. To Reseda High School on the west coast, I want to thank my coaches for giving me an opportunity to improve my skills to become a collegiate athlete.

To Santa Monica College and Coach McMullen, my teammates, especially Troy Baptise, R.I.P. That was my guy!! Shout out to Memorial Gym and Mooch for letting me put work in and make a name for myself out west. To the greatest HBCU on earth, THE Grambling State University, words cannot explain my love, appreciation, and gratitude for everything you have meant to my life academically, athletically, socially, spiritually, and everything in between. From Coach Eddie G. Robinson, my grandfather's college teammate, to the custodian who made sure my office remained in tip-top condition. Without GSU, I know I would not be the person I am today.

To my brothers of Benjamin E. Lewis Lodge #58, especially my line brothers 'FIST' and Guy Coleman, R.I.P., I love each and every one of you. To my brothers of the greatest fraternity on earth, Omega Psi Phi Fraternity Incorporated, especially Da Ruff Riders, my line brothers, much love. To my 5 KA, I love you 102019.

To my mother, sisters, nieces, nephews, aunts, uncles, cousins, and extended family, I love you all for loving me. Lena May Bivens, R.I.P. (Receiving Internal Prayers). Not a day goes by that I do not feel your presence, and I thank you with all my heart.

To my seeds, Princess, Zeek, MaMa, and Boaz, this is for you. Always remember that I may not have been there physically all the time, but each of you are the reason I live and have lived long enough to complete this book. I live by this motto, *The only fingerprint that cannot be removed is the one on the life that you touch.* I pray this book touches and changes a life!

My life in pictures...

My life in pictures...

My life in pictures...

My life in pictures...

My life in pictures...

My life in pictures...

My life in pictures...

My life in pictures...

Printed in the USA
CPSIA information can be obtained
at www.ICGtesting.com
CBHW050724110524
8339CB00010B/85